PRAISE FOR *PLANT-BASED ON A BUDGET*

"It's an unfortunate misconception that plant-based eating requires extravagant spending—nothing could be further from the truth, as *Plant-Based on a Budget* so expertly demonstrates. This book is an excellent resource for anyone who wants to make the healthiest choices possible while also spending wisely."

—T. Colin Campbell, PhD, coauthor of international bestseller
The China Study and *New York Times* bestseller *Whole*

"When I became a vegan in 1987, I was making $2,500 a year and spending $10 a week on food. And amazingly, I ate well! This book shows how easy it is to eat well and be a vegan without spending a ton of money."

—Moby, singer and songwriter

"Toni Okamoto is both a whiz in the kitchen and a whiz with her pocket book. In this masterful new cookbook, Okamoto makes plant-based eating delicious, easy, and affordable. *Plant-Based on a Budget* completely debunks the myth that eating healthy means having to spend a lot of money. Author Toni Okamoto provides all of the tips, tricks, and recipes you need to transform your kitchen, bank account, and life. Banana Zucchini Pancakes? Check. Coconut Curry Soup? Check. Four-Ingredient Chocolate Pie? Yes, please! We can't wait to make Toni's sumptuous, plant-based recipes—all at just a few dollars a piece. Want to be vibrantly healthy while staying on a budget? This is the book for you."

—Colleen Holland, publisher and cofounder of *VegNews*

"Toni Okamoto gives you the truth what too many large health charities are afraid to: Eating a plant-based diet can help save your life. She also shows you how it can save your finances, too."

—Kip Andersen, cocreator of *What the Health*

"Finally, a book made for people who want to save money while they save animals! These easy, affordable, recipes are great for big families like mine!"

—Alex Blue Davis, actor on *Grey's Anatomy*

D1268696

"Compassion doesn't have to cost an arm and a leg! In fact, Toni Okamoto shows that by letting animals keep their arms and legs, you can also keep more of your hard-earned dough in your pocket. Get her book!"

—Colleen Patrick-Goudreau, author and speaker

"Toni has been living and breathing budget-friendly living for more than a decade, and her knowledge and passion shines through in every page of this book. I had no idea just how much I was spending on food until I started applying Toni's money-saving tips. With this guide by my side, I cut my monthly food budget in half."

—Michelle Cehn, founder and content director of World of Vegan

"Plant-based eating has never been easier—or more affordable--than now. Buy this book and let Toni Okamoto help you keep your stomach and wallet full at the same time."

—Klaus Mitchell and Robbie Lockie, cofounders of Plant Based News

"Eating plants saves animals, and Toni Okamoto expertly shows you how it can save you money, too."

—Gene Baur, *New York Times* bestselling author of *Living the Farm Sanctuary Life* and *Farm Sanctuary*

"Whether or not you've got money growing on the trees in your life, if health is wealth—and I believe it is—than this book will give you the great gift of wealth that you deserve."

—Dr. Michael Greger, *New York Times* bestselling author of *How Not to Die*

PLANT-BASED
on a Budget

PLANT-BASED
on a Budget

Delicious **Vegan Recipes** for Under $30

a Week, in Less Than 30 Minutes a Meal

Toni Okamoto

BenBella Books, Inc.

Dallas, TX

BenBella Books, Inc.
10440 N. Central Expressway, Suite 800
Dallas, TX 75231
www.benbellabooks.com
Send feedback to feedback@benbellabooks.com

BenBella is a federally registered trademark.

Printed in the United States of America
10 9 8 7

Library of Congress Cataloging-in-Publication Data:
Names: Okamoto, Toni, author.
Title: Plant-based on a budget : delicious vegan recipes for under $30 a
week, in less than 30 minutes a meal / Toni Okamoto.
Description: Dallas, TX : BenBella Books, Inc., [2019] | Includes
bibliographical references and index.
Identifiers: LCCN 2018045421 (print) | LCCN 2018045559 (ebook) | ISBN
9781948836241 (electronic) | ISBN 9781946885982 (trade paper : alk. paper)
Subjects: LCSH: Vegetarian cooking. | Cooking (Natural foods) | One-dish
meals. | LCGFT: Cookbooks.
Classification: LCC TX837 (ebook) | LCC TX837 .O393 2019 (print) | DDC
641.5/636--dc23
LC record available at https://lccn.loc.gov/2018045421

Editing by Maria Teresa Hart
Copyediting by Jennifer Brett Greenstein
Proofreading by Amy Zarkos and Cape Cod Compositors, Inc.
Indexing by WordCo Indexing Services
Text design and composition by Aaron Edmiston
Food photography by Jenny Love
Lifestyle photography by Michelle Cehn
Cover design by Oceana Garceau
Printed by Versa Press

Distributed to the trade by Two Rivers Distribution, an Ingram brand
www.tworiversdistribution.com

Special discounts for bulk sales are available. Please contact bulkorders@benbellabooks.com.

To my business partner, Michelle, and my life partner, Paul. Thank you for carrying me through the depths of entrepreneurship and life, and for believing in me so much that I began to believe in myself. This book is a reality because of your love, encouragement, and support.

CONTENTS

FOREWORD

Unlike the fruits and veggies we know we should be eating, money sadly doesn't grow on trees or plants. If it did, we could all afford to eat healthy, right?

Well, I've got good news: We *can* all afford to eat healthy, and *Plant-Based on a Budget* shows you how. Whether you're a prince (or princess) or a pauper, you can enjoy the benefits of the diet science shows optimizes our health and reduces our risk of dying prematurely: a whole-foods, plant-based diet.

In other words, to eat plant-based, you don't need to shop at natural foods stores or dine on expensive acai bowls while sipping on whatever the bank-busting superfood-elixir-of-the-month happens to be. The supermarket you already shop at likely has everything you need to do right by both your body and your budget.

When I wrote *How Not to Die*, I wanted to share the latest science, which demonstrates that the illnesses that plague us the most are often preventable. With simple dietary changes, we can avoid subjecting ourselves to the chronic suffering and early death that the standard American diet (SAD) entails. At the same time, it's crucial for us to recognize that while diet-related illness affects us all, it often hits low-income communities the hardest.

For example, living in poverty is considered a major risk factor for heart disease, the number-one killer of Americans. When it comes to hypertension, one public health researcher told CNN: "When you look at this globally, blood pressure is a condition of poverty, not affluence." And if you're worried about diabetes, it helps to have money, since being poor is considered a leading factor that increases diabetes risk in America today.

The point is that those with low incomes are in need of the good news about plant-based eating the most. That's why I'm so enthusiastic about Toni Okamoto's work and this book in particular. Okamoto provides the road map for how to eat a whole-foods, plant-based diet while sticking to a strict budget. She's scoured the supermarkets to find the most affordable plant-based ingredients so you don't have to. And most importantly, she shows you exactly what to do with those ingredients to enjoy the most delicious ways of feeding yourself and your family.

You never thought you could eat healthy for less than two dollars per meal? Think again. With the right ingredients and recipes, you can feast off your own "dollar menu" and leave the fast-food chains behind.

So enjoy this book not just for its beautiful photography. Enjoy the benefits it can bring to your life. Because good health shouldn't be reserved merely for those who can afford it; none of us should be suffering from preventable illnesses. None of us should be leaving our family and friends earlier than we must.

Whether or not you've got money growing on the trees in your life, if health is wealth—and I believe it is—then this book will give you the great gift of wealth that you deserve.

BON APPÉTIT!
MICHAEL GREGER, MD, FACLM

INTRODUCTION

I've spent my career (and the past ten years of my life) figuring out the best ways to save your pennies while eating healthy. If there's one thing I've learned along the way, it's that *everyone* loves saving money. With this book, I'm going to tackle the top concerns people have when it comes to food: cost, convenience, nutrition, and taste. My goal? Teaching you how to whip up a delicious and nutritious meal in under thirty minutes that even your junk-food-loving friends will love, using only ingredients that you can find at your nearest (conventional) grocery store. I know that sounds like mission impossible, but it's actually very, very possible if you follow my lead.

Whether you're budgeting because of a limited income or you're looking to put your pennies elsewhere (travel, home, your Amazon wish list), I want to help you lower your food expenses. Not only that, but I want to show you how fast cooking can be so you can get back to walking your dog, having coffee with friends, or reading books to your kids. These recipes will show you how to maximize your efficiency in the kitchen so you can get back to simply living your life.

So thank you for welcoming me into your kitchen. If you're just starting out, don't be intimidated. I didn't start out as an expert either. Like many, I arrived at affordable plant-based eating through a journey.

MY STORY

My vegan journey really started back in high school. I ran track (look at how cute I looked in my uniform!), and I lived off a typical standard American diet. There was a Taco Bell located directly across from my school, and every day I'd go there for lunch and buy my standard order: two beef tacos and a bean burrito. Then I'd go to track practice and run as fast as my body could handle—and get sick to my stomach every single time. My coach suggested that I stop eating Taco Bell before track practice. He

knew fast food didn't exactly equal optimal health and fitness. But he went a step further and suggested that I stop eating red meat to enhance my performance. So my journey to plant-based eating started solely for health purposes. If you'd told me back then that I'd become a professional expert and advocate of the vegan diet, I would have laughed. Loudly.

Becoming full-on vegetarian was a slow road for me that hit several bottlenecks and traffic jams thanks to various living circumstances. After high school, I moved out of my family's house into a room I shared with two other people. I worked two jobs, one at the mall and one as a nanny, and tried to squirrel every cent away and make it count. Food wasn't a priority. I ate whatever free food anyone served me. But when I did go shopping, I only bought vegetarian food.

In my early twenties, I took some community college classes and joined the vegetarian club there. That's when my interest in plant-based eating really ramped up. That club became my support system, and the members really educated and inspired me. Together, we hosted bake sales, cooked potlucks, and visited farmed animal sanctuaries. Having that community made all the difference in my embrace of a plant-based, vegan lifestyle. Now I was a vegan not just for my health but for the larger causes of animal welfare and the environment. (The photo below, taken in 2008, shows me beaming as a newly minted vegan.)

My life changed pretty quickly after that. I had a new passion and purpose. I started working full-time doing social media and outreach for a farmed animal rescue. A couple of years after that, I started working for a vegan advocacy group. Those organizations helped me gain the experience and understanding of vegan advocacy work, and now I can't imagine doing anything else in my life.

That's my journey to veganism, but the path to being a food-budgeting expert also came from a lifetime of experience. Between low-paying jobs, car troubles, student loans, vet bills, and trying to pay down credit card debt, I've spent most of my adult life living paycheck to paycheck. For years, I'd look at my list of expenses and see the food grocery money fund being pushed to the bottom, because I knew that eating instant ramen everyday was better than being evicted.

I learned that type of survivalist mind-set from my parents. My dad was only nineteen when I was born, and for as far back as I can remember, he's made every financial decision to provide me with a comfortable life. He enlisted in the Navy to earn money that put food in my belly. I lived with my grandparents until I was eleven, when my dad used his VA loan to purchase a home in a safe neighborhood with a good school district. That year, I remember sitting on lawn chairs in our living room watching football with my family on Thanksgiving. We couldn't afford the traditional holiday-meal fixings, but my dad served us whatever food we had, knowing that his children had better opportunities in life because of his hard work.

It's fair to say that my family didn't spend a lot of money on food while I was growing up, so when I became a vegan in my early twenties, they were concerned that I'd be wasting every penny on my newfound vegan lifestyle. They thought I'd be shopping for weird and overpriced products at fancy-schmancy grocery stores where I had to pay to be a member (aka co-ops), quenching my thirst at organic juice bars, and using whatever was left in my wallet to do hippie-dippie things like getting my chakras aligned.

I quickly realized that a lot of people in my social circles and in my community felt the same way as my parents. I spent my childhood in a primarily Mexican American neighborhood, with many first- or second-generation families that were still establishing themselves in this country. My neighbors didn't have a lot of money to spend on food. Yet, in communities like mine, there was a plague of diet-related health problems like type 2 diabetes and heart disease.

Even my own family was suffering the side effects of unhealthy eating: my forty-year-old uncle had a heart attack, my aunt died after suffering through type 2 diabetes and multiple amputations, and my grandfather died from complications during a triple bypass surgery.

My goal was simple. I simply wanted to help my family stay alive. By this point, I'd been thriving on a vegan diet for years and wanted to share the positive effects with them. I knew I had to present the information in a way that was familiar and flavorful, and that addressed their biggest concern: cost.

Thus, Plant-Based on a Budget was officially born. Through my website and this book, I want to show you that you don't have to shop at expensive stores when you're vegan—you can shop at the most affordable grocery stores and still enjoy crazy-delicious plant-based cuisine.

HOW TO BE PLANT-BASED ON A BUDGET

When I first began my plant-based journey, I had no idea what I was doing. I didn't have cooking skills or money to shop for specialty ingredients, so I started checking out library books with basic recipes. One thing I noticed was that most budget-conscious cookbooks offer the tip that "eating less meat" will cut your grocery bill. I took that a step further and threw out eggs and dairy, too. I knew it was a step toward a healthy body and a healthy bank account.

To bring down the cost of groceries even more, I'd host potluck-style dinners where I'd invite friends, each with an assigned ingredient to bring, and then we'd all share in the cooking. It was during that time that I began experimenting with food, swapping out ingredients in recipes for items I had in my pantry, often to save on a more expensive item. Recipes are general guides—don't be afraid to experiment, swap out veggies or spices, use rice instead of quinoa, or use frozen instead of fresh. That's how I'm setting up this book. I'll give you the base of a good recipe, but I want you to play with it. The "Testers' Tips" throughout this book will give you some tweaks you can try, and the blank sections, "My Tips," will give you a space to add your own.

Kitchen Equipment

Starting out as a novice cook, I had a big pot and a little pot (neither of which had lids), a serving spoon, some mismatched dishes, a knife I'd purchased used from a thrift store, an IKEA cutting board, some old hummus containers I used for food storage, and some other odds and ends that my parents gave me when I moved out. Over time, I've improved my cookware with thrift-store finds, and much as I'd like an All-Clad set of pots and pans, I've found that my upgraded-but-still-used collection works just fine.

There's no need to invest in loads of fancy cookware when you're just getting started. You might have to skip a few recipes in my book if you don't have a food processor or a pot with a lid, but there will be *plenty* of other recipes you can try. If you're starting with an empty kitchen, do what I did: take a trip to IKEA or your local thrift store and buy yourself a cutting board, a vegetable peeler, a can opener, and a few pots and pans of different sizes with lids—I recommend a big soup pot and a small to medium pot. Go on Amazon, where you can pick up a decently rated kitchen knife for about six dollars. Go to Dollar Tree and buy some plastic storage containers. And if you have any cash after those purchases, buy a colander, basic kitchen utensils, and some different-sized bowls.

If you have all of the above and you're looking to level up your kitchen gear, I recommend an Instant Pot to help you quickly pressure-cook all your staples, a Vitamix to help you do things like make your own peanut butter, and a food processor to cut your vegetables and save you time. You can see some of the things I keep stocked in my kitchen at PlantBasedonaBudget .com/shop.

How to Save Money on Food

Thanks to working on Plant-Based on a Budget full-time, I've gotten money-saving tips down to a science. My best tip: give yourself permission to be cost-conscious with your food. I'll take the time to bust out the calculator app on my phone while going through my clipped coupons in the grocery store. And I'm not ashamed to hand an item back to the cashier at the register because I realized it's out of my budget. I learned this shamelessness as a child. I vividly remember on several occasions my dad holding up the line at the grocery store to ensure he got the sale price. When I'd tell him that people behind us were getting annoyed, he'd always say, "I don't care; they don't pay my bills." And that's how I feel now. If you're having trouble giving yourself permission to be cost conscious, or if you're feeling some embarrassment, just channel your inner George Okamoto.

Here are some of my best suggestions for stretching your dollar:

1. **Bring Measuring Cups for Bulk Purchases:** It may look a little silly, but this has saved me so much money. When you create your meal plan and grocery list for the week, note exactly how many cups or tablespoons of an ingredient your recipe needs. When you get to the grocery store, take a plastic produce bag and wrap a measuring cup so it's sanitary. Then head to the bulk bins and measure out exactly what you need. This prevents unnecessary spending and also saves space in your cupboard.

2. **Scrape Your Bowls:** Leave no leftovers behind! Have a little bit of tomato sauce left over in the can? Freeze it and throw it in a soup. Do you have some leftover pasta on your plate? Add it to your lunch tomorrow. Every bean or lentil or piece of rice adds up. I try to avoid throwing

any food away, because it feels like I'm tossing money directly into the trash can.

3. **Go to Farmers Markets:** Produce prices at farmers markets can vary (and truthfully, in some areas they can be expensive), but these are places where you can do some haggling. It's best to negotiate prices right before the market ends. The selection may not be as good, but the farmers aren't interested in lugging back what's left, so you're usually able to score a deal.

4. **Scout Out Imperfect Produce:** There are online companies selling produce for up to 50 percent cheaper than grocery stores because it doesn't meet their cosmetic standards. Do a quick Google search to see what's available in your area.

5. **Bring a Shopping List:** This tip is well-known for a reason. Shopping with intention helps cut back on impulse purchases and keeps you within your budget. I like to tally all the items I already have on hand, then make a list of whatever else I need and take that to the store.

6. **Check Out Bulk Foods and Spices:** When exploring your area for the best grocery store, consider the options that have bulk bins. These bins allow you to purchase as much or as little as you need, and they're especially cost saving when shopping for spices.

7. **Cook from Scratch:** At the grocery store, I walk right pass the frozen vegan pizzas and remember that I can make five pizzas from scratch for the same cost. Cooking from scratch often gives you double or triple the amount of food for the same price. Plus, it allows you more flexibility to tailor your food to suit your preferences.

8. **Keep Food Prepared:** Any time I get really busy, Chipotle and Subway become even more

enticing as quick solutions to my hunger. To avoid the crutch of fast food, I try to keep to-go snacks with me at all times. I keep peanuts in my glove compartment or some Five-Ingredient Peanut Butter Bites (see page 26) in my purse.

9. **Check Price per Ounce:** At first glance, two cans of tomato sauce may have the same price, but on closer inspection, you spot that one can is larger. When doing a price comparison, make sure you're looking at the price per ounce instead of the unit price, which is often displayed on the price tag in the supermarket.

10. **Look at the Whole Aisle:** Like any other store, grocery stores are pushing their products to make a profit. They spotlight "sale" items on the endcaps of the aisle, offering up a deal. But when you go to the section where those products belong, you'll often find that there are cheaper options. Also, they place more expensive options at eye level, since many people don't take the time to look up or down to see what's cheaper.

11. **Buy Store Brands:** Often the store's own brand is the cheapest option, and these products are just as good as the major-label product. Sometimes, it actually is the same major-label product with the grocery store's private label slapped on it.

12. **Freeze Your Produce Before It Expires:** Are your bananas getting spotty? Peel them, chop them, throw them in a freezer bag, and toss them in the freezer. I do the same with mangoes, peaches, berries, and so on. If you're trying to reduce your use of plastic while saving a few pennies, reuse those freezer bags by washing them with soap and water and letting them air-dry. You can also buy reusable silicone bags on Amazon, which I *love* because they're dishwasher friendly.

13. **Scope Out Several Stores:** The closest grocery store may not be the cheapest. Always, always shop around to scout out a few options. Visit your local international markets, check out the big-box warehouse grocery stores, and even see what's for sale at the dollar stores. You'll be surprised how cheap some of your favorite products may be.

14. **Clip Coupons:** When I was younger, my mom had an accordion folder with written tabs that organized her coupons. These days, all you need to do is download the app from your favorite stores to digitally clip their coupons. When you're at the register, have the clerk scan your app barcode. It's so easy and much more discreet than it used to be. You can score big at stores like Target, Sprouts, and even Whole Foods. Also, be sure to sign up for email from your favorite grocery stores to get the scoop on their sales and mobile coupons. If your inbox is overloaded, start an email account called something like "toniscoupons@gmail.com" so grocery email doesn't spam your regular account, and check it when you go on a grocery run.

15. **Cook with Friends:** As mentioned earlier, this was a cost-saving tip I used when I first started cooking, and it's a win-win for everyone, because both the labor and expense of making a meal are shared. I still do this. For example, at Thanksgiving, we have a potluck so one person doesn't get stuck cooking everything. We choose a recipe, divide the ingredients, and make big batches for people to take home. I love this because it not only saves you money but also provides an opportunity to bond and break bread together.

16. **Double Up on Sales:** If you have the pantry/fridge space and you see your favorite products on

sale, stock up. Do double-check check the expiration dates to make sure you have time to finish the items before they go bad.

17. **Stock Up on Frozen Veggies:** "Eat more vegetables" is a common dietary resolution. We'll stock up on greens and then our schedules will get in the way, leaving everything to wilt in the fridge. Buying frozen produce fixes that. Or, if you see produce that is on a super sale, buy it and freeze it yourself.

18. **Eat Leftovers:** Once you've gotten those food storage containers from the thrift store or IKEA, put them to use. When I'm meal planning, I cook four big meals to last the entire week. Bonus: not only does this save me cash, but it also saves me time in the kitchen.

19. **Splurge on Something Small:** Yes, I can and do splurge, and I consider it part of my plan. I want to set myself up for long-term success in healthy,

plant-based eating, and I'm more likely to stick to it if I don't feel 100 percent deprived. Personally, I make sure to get myself a sweet or salty treat when I go shopping. It may be an item like a small bag of potato chips or a snack pack of Nutter Butters to munch on over the next week.

20. **Repurpose Food:** I'm forever trying to figure out ways to reuse food. Dislike bread heels? Turn them into bread crumbs or croutons (see page 233). Or have some cooked quinoa you're not getting to fast enough? Freeze it and throw it in your next soup or chili.

21. **Store Your Herbs Properly:** Cooking with fresh herbs takes your dishes to the next level, but often herbs go bad in the refrigerator before you have a chance to use them. To lengthen their lifespan, trim the stems, stick them in a cup of water, and cover the cup and herbs with the plastic bag they

came in. Just like cut flowers, herbs last longer in water.

22. **Be Mindful of Expiration Dates:** Every time you throw away expired food, picture yourself throwing dollar bills in the trash can. Because that is what you're doing. To avoid that awful reality, be conscious of what you have and what date it needs to be used by. When you plan your meals, use up what will expire first. Sometimes it's helpful to literally write dates on sticky notes and stick them on the food in your fridge.

23. **Bake Bread:** Did you know that you can bake bread using only four ingredients? It's really cheap—much cheaper than buying it at the grocery store—and seriously delicious. If you're new to bread baking, check out the great recipe someone posted on PlantBasedonaBudget.com called "Free Formed Bread."

24. **Ask for Cheaper Deals:** Sometimes grocery stores will give discounts on bruised or imperfect produce. I've gotten bananas for twenty-five cents per pound just by asking, and the only thing wrong with them was a few brown spots. Find a store employee in the produce section and ask if there is any discounted ripened produce available. It's always worth a try.

25. **Check the Clearance Section:** Next time you're at Target or Walmart, swing by the clearance section. I've found spices for under a dollar and olive oil for two dollars.

26. **Buy Only What You Need:** Some people love the feeling of abundance they get from having a fully stocked refrigerator. But buying food just to fill out your fridge can also create food waste when you don't use it up. Don't feel pressured to keep every shelf and crisper drawer stocked. Instead, create a meal plan before you shop and buy only what you plan on using.

27. **Freeze Sauces When Produce Is in Season:** Apart from freezing whole fruits and veggies, a great time and money saver is to freeze sauces. Add the sauces to an ice cube tray, freeze them, and place those cubes in a freezer bag for use throughout the year. That summer-garden pesto? The marinara from your farmers market tomatoes? You'll be able to enjoy them weeks after their season ends.

28. **Watch the Screen While They're Ringing You Up:** It's good to pay attention when your items are being scanned or keyed in, especially when you're buying bulk items. I've accidentally written the wrong number and caught the cashier charging me extra. Thanks to keeping an eye on the register, I was able to get the price corrected before it went on my credit card.

29. **Stock Up After Holidays:** For the budget-conscious, the postholiday season is like Christmas all over again. That's when the prices for themed items drop by 70 percent. It's a great time to stock up. I like to buy cupcake liners for my breakfast muffins and ziplock bags for storage. I don't mind that they feature snowmen and Santa as long as they're saving me money.

30. **Grow Your Own:** If you have a backyard and can afford to plant a fruit tree, definitely do it. A healthy tree can provide you with fruit for decades. You can plant a backyard garden in planter boxes or grow a container garden on your porch. Don't have either? Grow some fresh herbs in your kitchen. My mom, who had no gardening experience, began a small backyard garden a few years ago from seeds. She told me she saves hundreds of dollars in produce every year.

How to Save Time

A common misconception about me is that cooking is my number-one passion. The honest truth is I love eating, and cooking is a means to a (delicious) end. I'd much rather be spending time with loved ones, building my career, enjoying the outdoors, or having a million other enriching experiences. I strongly believe that time is the most valuable asset in our lives. Because of this, I want to share the time-budgeting tips I've discovered over the years.

1. **Plan Your Meals:** Use your Sunday to plan your meals for the week. That way, when your brain is exhausted after work, you don't spend half an hour opening and closing the fridge and cupboard doors, trying to figure out what you can piece together.

2. **Buy Jarred Minced Garlic:** I'd walked by jarred garlic a million times at the grocery store without thinking twice. It wasn't until I was writing my last book, in which all the prep time for recipes was done in under fifteen minutes, that I realized its supreme convenience. To me, it tastes the same, plus you don't have to fuss around with peeling and mincing.

3. **Get a Garlic Press:** Skeptical about jarred garlic? If you *really* love fresh garlic and don't want to risk compromising any flavor, you can still save time by using a garlic press instead of mincing by hand. Yet again, IKEA came through for me with an inexpensive and good-quality press that I've had for a decade.

4. **Stock Up on Frozen Veggies:** Not only do frozen veggies have a longer expiration date, but they're also already precut. I always keep my freezer stocked with broccoli, peas, cauliflower,

and whatever other frozen veggies are on sale.

5. **Get Your Family Involved:** If you live with your family or have roommates, get them to join in on the fun of cooking. Put the kids in charge of washing the veggies, have your partner chop produce, and you can make the magic on the stovetop. You can also have the arrangement that I have in my home: I cook and the eaters do the dishes.

6. **Invest in a Slow Cooker:** If you're on a tight budget, I recommend visiting a thrift store and finding a slow cooker. I picked up my 1970s floral burnt orange slow cooker at Goodwill for four dollars. I love that I can cook my beans in it while I sleep; throw in some veggies, canned tomatoes, and spices before work; and have a meal waiting for me at the end of the day. Minimal effort and maximum flavor.

7. **Consider a Pressure Cooker:** If you have some spending money, purchasing a pressure cooker will change your life. I purchased my Instant Pot used on Amazon. It came with a huge dent on the side that didn't disturb its functionality, and I got thirty dollars off. Now, I have quinoa in five minutes, beans in one hour, and my favorite, soup, in five minutes.

8. **Learn to Love Leftovers:** Batch cooking is my jam! I only want to cook full meals two or three times a week, so when I am

already in the kitchen, I make it count. I will double or triple my batches so that I can have leftovers for lunch. Very rarely do I have to think about what I am going to eat for lunch because I often have leftovers.

9. **Double Up on Your Prep:** When you're chopping for a recipe, chop some other vegetables while you have your knife and cutting board out. If you're cutting an onion, chop two of them and throw one in a container to use later in the week.

10. **Buy Canned Beans:** I love a good batch of homemade beans, but unfortunately my schedule doesn't always allow me to make them as often as I want to eat them. That's why I try to make sure my pantry is stocked with a variety of canned beans. (I like pinto beans, black beans, and chickpeas.) On days when I am ultra-busy, I can take a can of beans, some store-bought salsa, and a chopped

avocado and wrap them up in a burrito to have a quick and easy meal.

11. **Clean as You Go:** Cleaning up is the least fun part of cooking, but I find it's much more manageable to do as you go along. Rather than waiting until the next morning, when the food is all dried and stuck to the plates, rinse it off and wash the dishes immediately after use. That will definitely save you scrubbing time.

12. **Plan Your Shopping Route:** When writing your grocery shopping list, try to remember to organize it by grocery store section. When I do mine, I organize it under headings such as "produce," "bulk," "frozen," and "other." This stops me from taking multiple unnecessary trips back and forth across the grocery store and makes my shopping experience much more efficient.

13. **No More Peeling:** Stop peeling your carrots, cucumbers,

potatoes, zucchini, and so on. Not only will you be saving time by doing this, but you'll also be saving all the nutrients that are stored in the peels.

14. **Meal Swap with Friends:** Have a friend at work who likes to cook? Work out a deal where once a week each of you will double-batch a meal and bring the extra to work the next morning for a trade. Maybe you can even gift your friend this cookbook to ensure that what you're getting is healthy and plant-based. ;-)

15. **Keep Bouillon Handy:** If you don't want to make your own vegetable broth (see page 242), keep a couple of packages of vegetarian bouillon in your pantry. You can also keep a jar of Better Than Bouillon.

16. **Prep Breakfast Beforehand:** Mornings are a hectic time. Make life easier by preparing in advance. You can either prepare something like Overnight Oats (see page 36) or put your smoothie fixings in a storage container so that in the morning all you have to do is dump them in the blender with some plant-based milk.

17. **Invest in a Good Knife:** For years, I used a hand-me-down set of Walmart knives and ones that I got from thrift stores. They were all serrated but dull knives, and it'd take me minutes to cut a carrot. I didn't even know there was another way because those were the knives that I grew up with in my home. Recently, I finally invested in a set of six Cuisinart knives on Amazon for twenty dollars, and now I whiz through those vegetables.

18. **Get to Know Your Kitchen:** The more time you spend in your kitchen, the less time you'll spend opening up random drawers trying to remember where you keep your vegetable peeler. In my kitchen, every item has a home so I waste no

time looking around for where it is.

19. **Make Dry Mixes:** If you have time on the weekend, prep some muffin or pancake mixes to easily whip together on your busier days. Attach a sticky note saying what you still need to add. For example, if you make pancake mix, write, "still need to add 1 cup plant-based milk."

20. **Use a Compost Bowl:** Keep a bowl for food scraps near your knife and cutting board. Don't waste time or energy walking back and forth to the trash can. If you're cutting veggies, you can save the scraps for a veggie broth (see page 242), or you can throw the unusable food waste straight into a yard waste bin so it doesn't make your trash can stink.

Cooking Basics and Notes About This Book

Here's a little extra information and clarification to make the recipes ahead even easier.

1. **Freezing Bananas:** The first time I ever froze bananas, I didn't know I was supposed to peel them first. When I went to use them, the peelings were impossible to remove. Learn from my mistake: when your bananas are ripe (the browner, the better), peel them, thinly slice them, and put them in a freezer bag or storage container in the freezer.

2. **Pressing Tofu:** This is far simpler than it sounds. Here's how to press it like a pro: slice open the package of tofu with a knife, pour out the water, slice the tofu, and wrap each slice in a clean kitchen towel while pressing the excess

water out, which is absorbed by the kitchen towel. That's all. Just get the excess water out. People also use paper towels to do it, but it's wasteful and costs more money, so I stick to clean kitchen towels. You can also wrap the tofu in a towel and put something heavy on it like a book to press it for a few minutes while you prep other things.

3. **Making Vegetable Broth:** I exclusively use richly flavored bouillon cubes when I cook, and I mostly do a 2:1 ratio of cups of water to bouillon cubes. You're welcome to use low-sodium broth, but remember that it won't be as flavorful, and you may want to add some other spices to make up for it. You can also use the broth on page 242.

4. **Using Water Versus Oil:** There's a huge spectrum of cooking preferences and my audience includes all of them. To cater to everyone, I have added both oil options and no-oil options to recipes in which ingredients are sautéed. If you don't use oil, in every recipe that calls for oil for sautéing, you can swap each tablespoon of oil for 3 tablespoons of water.

5. **Rinsing Beans and Grains Well:** One time I was doing a "What I Eat in a Day" video on my YouTube channel and bit into a pebble that had made its way into my split pea soup. I even showed the offending pebble in my video. That's to say, it's important to rinse your staples like beans, lentils, quinoa, and split peas before you use them.

6. **Steaming Veggies:** When I started cooking, I only knew how to boil veggies, so I want to make sure I give you some instruction on how to steam. If you can afford it, I recommend picking up a steamer basket to put in your pot with a lid. Then you'll fill your steamer basket with your choice of veggies, make sure there's water in your

pot, cover it, and steam for 3 to 5 minutes or until your veggies are tender. If you don't have a steamer basket but you have a pot with a lid, you can "steep" your veggies in a little bit of water. That means add your veggies and enough water to cover the bottom of the pot, cover with a lid, and cook on low for 5 minutes or until the veggies are tender.

7. **Using Salt and Pepper, to Taste:** As I mentioned, my audience drastically varies in taste preference, so I'm leaving the sodium up to you. What "to taste" means in my recipes is add salt until it tastes good to you. That said, if you're a big salt lover, I recommend reducing the amount of salt you use, and I promise your palate will change to accommodate this. And your body will thank you.

8. **"Testers' Tips":** It was important to me to have a diverse group of people testing my recipes. They were spread out all over the country and varied in age by about fifty years. Some were expert chefs and some never cooked. And most were not vegan—or even vegetarian. I'm thrilled with the wonderful, detailed feedback they offered, and I tried to share as many of their insights as I could.

9. **"My Tips":** If you flipped through my cookbook collection, you'd find that I scribbled all over them. I wrote which days I made certain recipes, how they were modified based on ingredients I had handy, and whether or not I'd make them again. I've had some of my cookbooks for over a decade, and I still refer to the notes I made back then. That's why I included "My Tips"—to encourage you to do the same. I really want this book to be something that has food splattered all over it and is all marked up, because that's an indication you've really put this book to use. Make my recipes your own.

My Vegan Cooking Staples

My goal with this book is to help you spend the least amount of time and energy in the kitchen, while still serving delicious and nutritious meals. To help you cut some corners on time, I've given you time-saving tips for cooking and stocking your kitchen. Now I'm taking that a step further and giving you a quick grocery list you can take to the store to stock up on all the basics.

Note that if you prefer using homemade beans and fresh produce, that is totally fine. The recipes I provide are designed to keep prep time to a minimum, but all of them are flexible and easily modified—just make sure to budget extra time for cooking and prep if you're using different ingredients. And note that one can of beans is about 1½ cups.

Affordable Dry Staples

Barley

Beans (black beans, pinto beans, and chickpeas)

Brown rice

Bulgur wheat

Corn tortillas

Flour (whole wheat and all-purpose)

Oats

Pasta

Raisins

Raw sunflower seeds

Red or green lentils

Vegetable bouillon

Canned or Bottled Goods

Chopped tomatoes

Coconut milk

Hot sauce

Oil (olive and canola or vegetable)

Peanut butter

Plant-based milk

Soy sauce

Tomato paste

Tomato sauce

Fruits and Veggies

Bananas

Bell peppers (green)

Butternut squash

Cabbage (green and red)

Fresh greens (lettuce, spinach, or kale)

Frozen broccoli

Frozen or fresh berries

Frozen peas

Frozen spinach

Jarred minced garlic

Onions (red, white, and yellow)

Potatoes (russet and sweet potatoes)

Spices

Cinnamon

Chili powder

Cumin

Curry powder

Oregano

Pepper

Red chili flakes

Salt

Staples for When You Splurge

Dried fruit (cranberries, coconut shreds, apricots, blueberries, etc.)

Nutritional yeast

Nuts and pumpkin seeds

Quinoa

BANANA ZUCCHINI PANCAKES

Yields 8 medium pancakes

About a decade ago, my best friend and roommate at the time (hi, Candice!) loaned me the book *Deceptively Delicious* by Jessica Seinfeld. Although I'd adopted veganism and couldn't eat almost anything in the book, I did learn about deceptively, deliciously packing food with vegetables. To get her children to eat healthier, Seinfeld would grate or purée veggies and add them to their favorite foods. That's where I got the idea to do that in my own food. Adding grated zucchini gives a nutritional boost without adding a veggie taste.

Ingredients:
1 cup whole wheat or all-purpose flour
2 teaspoons baking powder
½ teaspoon salt
2 tablespoons canola or vegetable oil, plus more for greasing
1 mashed banana
¼ cup grated zucchini (about 1 small zucchini)
1 cup plant-based milk
1½ teaspoons vanilla extract
1 tablespoon agave, brown sugar, or maple syrup

Optional Additions:
½ teaspoon cinnamon added in step 2
½ tablespoon flaxseed meal added in step 2

Optional Toppings:
Sliced bananas
Vegan butter
Maple syrup or maple agave

Directions:

1. Preheat a nonstick pan over medium-high heat. If you don't have a nonstick pan (or your nonstick pan needs a bit more slip), you can lightly oil the pan.

2. In a medium bowl, mix together all the ingredients. Gently mix until the batter is smooth, but there's no need to remove all the lumps.

3. Scoop out the batter with a ¼-cup measuring cup and pour onto the preheated pan. Once bubbles begin to form in the center of the pancake, flip the pancake over and cook the other side until light brown. Remove from the heat and repeat until all the batter is cooked.

TONI'S TIPS:

>>Pancakes are tough to get right. Make sure you start off with a preheated pan; if you don't, it will be difficult to flip the pancake and your first one or two will look funky. Try not to overmix the batter—the more you mix, the tougher they'll be.

>>To keep the pancakes warm while you're cooking, place the finished ones on a baking sheet in a warm oven set at 200 degrees.

MY TIPS:

TOFU SCRAMBLE

Yields 4 servings

Whenever I'm hosting brunch, this is my go-to recipe. Since I grew up eating scrambled eggs, this was a normal swap when I became vegan. It's super tasty, and there's no cholesterol.

Ingredients:

½ tablespoon canola or vegetable oil
(or 3 tablespoons water)

½ cup diced green or red bell pepper
(about ½ bell pepper)

½ cup diced red, white, or yellow onion
(about ½ medium onion)

1½ teaspoons minced garlic (about 3
small cloves)

1 (14-ounce) block extra-firm tofu,
pressed (see page 18)

2 teaspoons turmeric

2 cups chopped fresh or frozen spinach
or kale

Salt and pepper, to taste

Optional Additions:

½ cup diced potato added in step 1

1 teaspoon vegan butter added in step 3

¼ cup nutritional yeast added in step 3

½ cup grated carrot added in step 3

1 cup frozen broccoli added in step 3

1 sliced zucchini added in step 3

Directions:

1. In a large pan over medium heat, heat the oil (or water). Add the bell pepper, onion, and garlic, and sauté for 5 to 7 minutes or until the bell pepper and onion are tender.
2. Using your fingers, crumble the tofu into the pan.
3. Add the turmeric to the tofu and veggies and mix thoroughly.
4. Mix in the spinach (or kale). Cook for another 5 minutes, stirring occasionally.
5. Sprinkle with salt and pepper.

TONI'S TIPS:

>>The scramble is definitely good as it is, but it is *great* with the nutritional yeast. If you want to splurge, I definitely recommend adding it. If you want it to coat the mixture evenly, add a little vegan butter with it.

MY TIPS:

BLUEBERRY BANANA MUFFINS

Yields 6 muffins

Blueberry muffins are my absolute favorite. Whip up a batch of these over the weekend and enjoy them throughout the week.

Ingredients:

1½ cups mashed ripe bananas (about 3 medium bananas)

¼ cup granulated sugar

⅓ cup canola or vegetable oil, plus more for greasing

1 teaspoon baking powder

1 teaspoon baking soda

½ teaspoon salt

1½ cups whole wheat or all-purpose flour

1 cup fresh or frozen blueberries

Optional Additions:

1 teaspoon cinnamon added in step 3

1 tablespoon flaxseed meal added in step 3

Directions:

1. Preheat the oven to 375 degrees, and lightly grease a muffin tin.
2. Place the mashed bananas in a large bowl.
3. Add the sugar, oil, baking powder, baking soda, salt, and flour, and gently mix together until well combined.
4. Fold the blueberries into the batter.
5. Spoon the batter into the muffin tin, filling each cup to the top.
6. Bake for 25 minutes or until the muffins are golden brown.

TONI'S TIPS:

>> For a healthier (but less sweet) muffin, omit the sugar.

>> These muffins will keep in the refrigerator for up to 5 days. Pack them in an airtight container.

TESTERS' TIPS:

>> "Insert a toothpick in the middle of the muffin. If you pull it out and it's dry, you'll know it's finished baking."
—Melanie S. from Warsaw, NY

MY TIPS:

OVERNIGHT OATS

Yields 1 to 2 servings

In my home, we live off Overnight Oats. They're so crazy simple to put together! I like to prepare up to four days' worth at a time. I use my weekend to prep a few for the upcoming week, and it makes those busy weekday mornings that much easier to bear.

Ingredients:

1 cup old-fashioned rolled oats

¾ cup frozen berries

2 tablespoons raw sunflower seeds (no shells)

1 cup plant-based milk

1 banana, sliced

Optional Toppings:

1 teaspoon maple syrup

1 teaspoon brown sugar

1½ teaspoons cinnamon

1½ teaspoons chia seeds

1 tablespoon coconut flakes

Directions:

1. Add the oats, berries, sunflower seeds, and milk to a storage container, glass, or mason jar.
2. Cover with a lid or aluminum foil and refrigerate overnight.
3. In the morning, mix and enjoy chilled. (No cooking or heating is necessary—the oats soften overnight.)
4. Garnish with the sliced banana to sweeten.

TONI'S TIPS:

>>You can swap out the frozen berries for other fruit, or swap out the sunflower seeds for your favorite nuts or seeds.

TESTERS' TIPS:

>>"Mashing a banana into the oats while preparing them makes everything hearty and creamy in the morning." —Toube B. from Chico, CA

>>"It's also a great recipe with steel-cut oats. It's a bit more chewy, a tad 'under-cooked,' but in a good way. I would suggest cutting both the oats and plant-based milk in half for a steel-cut oat version." —Roxane M. from Neptune, NJ

>>"If you want your oatmeal warm, you can microwave it for a couple of minutes in the morning." —Melanie S. from Warsaw, NY

PUMPKIN BITES

Yields 12 bites

If you're looking for a healthy morning snack on the go with no added sugar, look no further than these perfect Pumpkin Bites.

Ingredients:
1 teaspoon canola or vegetable oil (for greasing)

2 cups old-fashioned rolled oats

¾ cup pumpkin purée

¾ cup unsweetened applesauce

1½ teaspoons cinnamon

½ cup coconut flakes

¾ cup raisins

Optional Additions:
½ teaspoon nutmeg added in step 3

¼ teaspoon ground cloves added in step 3

¼ cup chopped walnuts added in step 5

MY TIPS:

Directions:
1. Preheat the oven to 350 degrees, and lightly grease a muffin tin.
2. In a food processor, pulse the oats until they turn into a flour.
3. Add the pumpkin purée, applesauce, cinnamon, and coconut flakes.
4. Blend until the mixture becomes a smooth batter.
5. Add the raisins and stir by hand with a spoon.
6. Spoon the batter into the muffin tin, filling each cup halfway.
7. Bake for 18 to 20 minutes. Test by sticking a toothpick in the middle of a muffin. If the toothpick comes out dry, the muffins are done.

TONI'S TIPS:

>> These bites can keep for up to 5 days if they're stored in an airtight container in the fridge.

STOVETOP BLUEBERRY OATMEAL

Yields 1 to 2 servings

Whenever I'm planning a weekly menu for PlantBasedMealPlan.com, I always go back to serving oatmeal for breakfast because it's inexpensive, packed with nutrients, and quick and easy to make. I know that oatmeal can sound super boring, but there's so much potential for dressing it up. Add your favorite toppings and I promise it'll be a breakfast you come to crave.

Ingredients:

1½ cups plant-based milk

1 cup old-fashioned rolled oats

½ cup fresh or frozen blueberries

Optional Toppings:

1 tablespoon sweetener (agave, brown sugar, or maple syrup)

1 teaspoon spices of your choosing (like cinnamon or pumpkin pie spice)

2 tablespoons chopped nuts

2–3 tablespoons granola

1 tablespoon coconut shreds

2 tablespoons raw sunflower seeds (no shells)

Directions:

1. In a medium saucepan over medium-high heat, bring the milk to a boil.
2. Stir in the oats and frozen blueberries and reduce the heat to low.
3. Simmer for 5 minutes, stirring occasionally.
4. Remove from the heat and serve with optional toppings.

MY TIPS:

BREAKFAST QUINOA

Yields 2 to 4 servings

When I get sick of eating oats every day, I change it up by throwing Breakfast Quinoa into the mix. Since I try not to add a lot of sugar to my everyday recipes, I use only sliced banana to sweeten it up. If you want a sweeter dish, add some coconut shreds, raisins, dried cranberries, or mashed banana to the mix.

Ingredients:
2 cups plant-based milk
1 cup quinoa
½ cup frozen berries
1½ teaspoons cinnamon
1 banana, sliced

Optional Toppings:
Walnuts or almonds
Raw sunflower seeds (no shells)
Coconut shreds
Brown sugar

Directions:
1. In a medium pot over medium-high heat, bring the milk to a boil.
2. Reduce the heat to low, add the quinoa, and cover.
3. Let the quinoa simmer for 15 minutes. Add the frozen berries and cinnamon, stir, cover, and simmer for 5 more minutes. Remove from the heat.
4. Fluff the quinoa by mixing it with a spoon.
5. Serve with the sliced banana and any optional toppings.

TONI'S TIPS:

>> Save on time by cooking this in a pressure cooker. Throw everything into the pot except the berries, and cook on high pressure for 5 minutes. When it's done, mix in the berries. If you're using frozen berries, let them sit in the hot quinoa for 5 minutes to thaw out.

>> If you want to save money on this recipe, use 1 cup water and 1 cup milk instead of 2 cups milk.

"If the quinoa gets a little dry when it cools, add a splash of milk when serving." — Erica S. from Huntington Beach, CA

MY TIPS:

CHILAQUILES

Yields 2 to 4 servings

The word *chilaquiles* is derived from the Nahuatl (language of the Aztecs in Mexico) word *chil-a-quilitl*, which means "herbs or greens in chili broth." It's traditionally made with eggs and cheese, but since I no longer eat those things, I did my best to create a tasty plant-based version of one of my childhood-favorite Mexican dishes.

Ingredients:
2 tablespoons canola or vegetable oil

5 corn tortillas, cut into small strips

¾ cup diced red, white, or yellow onion (about 1 medium onion)

1 teaspoon minced garlic (about 2 small cloves)

1 (14-ounce) block extra-firm tofu, pressed (see page 18)

6 sprigs cilantro, chopped

1 tablespoon ground cumin

1 teaspoon chili powder

½ teaspoon salt

Pinch of pepper

1 (15-ounce) can pinto beans, drained and rinsed

1 batch Tomatillo Salsa (see page 98) or Homemade Red Salsa (see page 91) or a bottle of your favorite salsa

Optional Additions:
1 cup chopped spinach added in step 4

1 jalapeño, seeded and minced (if you like your salsa spicy), added in step 4

Optional Toppings:
Fresh or canned jalapeños

Sliced avocado

Directions:

1. In a large frying pan over medium-high heat, heat the oil and fry the tortilla strips for 1½ minutes on each side or until they are crispy.

2. Add the onion and garlic and sauté for 2 minutes or until the onion is tender and translucent.

3. Using your fingers, crumble the tofu into the pan.

4. Add the cilantro, cumin, chili powder, salt, and pepper, and cook on medium-high for 5 minutes, stirring frequently.

5. Add the pinto beans, mix well, and let cook for 2 more minutes.

6. Serve topped with the salsa.

TONI'S TIPS:

>>If the term *sprigs* is unfamiliar, here's a little helpful info: Cilantro is sold in bunches. Each bunch contains stems with cilantro leaves. Those are called sprigs.

>>If you're doubling this batch and planning on saving some for a later meal, when serving the leftovers it's best to start at step 2 and fry up new corn tortillas.

>>Use corn chips instead of frying the tortillas if you want to save on time.

TESTERS' TIPS:

>>"Vegan sour cream would be A+ in lieu of avocado. I also recommend ½ teaspoon turmeric for health and to make the tofu a yellow color, similar to the color of eggs." —Logan J. from Sacramento, CA

MY TIPS:

GREEN BANANA SMOOTHIE

Yields 2 large glasses

My first green smoothie came from a recipe by my friend Roxane McNulty. She was one of the initial recipe authors on PlantBasedonaBudget.com, and this is one of my favorite contributions on the whole website. I've slightly modified the measurements to bump up the sweetness, but you can find her original version on the website. Thanks again, Roxane, for giving us a tasty, healthy breakfast staple!

Ingredients:
2½–3 sliced frozen bananas
1½ cups spinach or kale, stems removed
1½ cups plant-based milk

Optional Additions:
1 tablespoon flaxseed meal added in step 1

Directions:
1. In a blender, blend all the ingredients on high until smooth.

TONI'S TIPS:
>>Make sure to check out my tips for freezing bananas on page 18.
>>If you like your smoothie even sweeter, use three frozen bananas.

TESTERS' TIPS:
>>"If you don't have a high-powered blender, blend the milk and kale together first to reduce any green chunks." —Melanie S. from Warsaw, NY

MY TIPS:

HOMEMADE GRANOLA CLUSTERS

Yields 2 cups

I have a special place in my heart for no-bake recipes because when weather is 110 degrees in Sacramento, the last thing I want to do is turn on my oven. And this is truly one of the best I've ever eaten. For this recipe, I used the cheapest seeds and dried fruit, but you can switch it up with pumpkin seeds or dried blueberries, or whatever else you love or have on hand.

Ingredients:
1½ cups peanut butter (creamy or chunky)
¼ cup agave or maple syrup
1½ cups old-fashioned rolled oats
¾ cup flaxseed meal
½ cup raisins
¾ cup raw sunflower seeds (no shells)

Optional Toppings:
¼ cup coconut shreds
1 teaspoon cinnamon
Pinch of salt

Directions:
1. Add the peanut butter and agave (or maple syrup) to a medium, microwave-safe bowl. Microwave on high for 30-second intervals, stirring between intervals until the mixture is creamy and well combined.
2. Add the oats, flaxseed meal, raisins, and sunflower seeds, and stir together with a spoon until thoroughly combined.
3. Transfer the mixture to a baking sheet.
4. Place in the freezer for at least 25 minutes. Store in the refrigerator in an airtight container for up to 7 days.

TONI'S TIPS:

>>This granola is a great topping for your favorite vegan yogurt or smoothie bowl.

HUMMUS AND AVOCADO BAGEL

Yields 1 serving

When I was younger and lived with my parents, my mom would buy bags of bagels for us as an easy breakfast before school. We'd smear cream cheese on top and be on our way. Since then, I've opted for this upgrade of my childhood favorite. I've replaced the cream cheese with two of my favorite toppings. And when I'm feeling fancy, I add some diced tomatoes and green sprouts.

Ingredients:

1 bagel

¼ serving of Homemade Hummus (see page 88) or store-bought hummus

½ avocado, sliced

Pinch of salt and pepper

Optional Toppings:

¼ cup diced tomatoes

1 handful finely diced red or green onion

Squeeze of lemon juice

1 handful sprouts

Directions:

1. Split the bagel in half. In a toaster or under the broiler, toast the bagel.
2. Spread the hummus on each side.
3. Top with the avocado, salt, and pepper.

MY TIPS:

SWEET POTATO BREAKFAST BOWL

Yields 1 to 2 servings

When I was a child, I thought the fast-food drive-through was the ultimate solution to busy mornings. This recipe taught me a better way. You can whip it together in minutes flat and start your day packed with nutrition.

Ingredients:

1 microwaved sweet potato, diced (see page 238)

1 teaspoon cinnamon

2 tablespoons raisins

1 tablespoon chopped pecans or walnuts

Optional Toppings:

1 tablespoon coconut shreds

Fresh berries

1 tablespoon peanut butter (creamy or chunky)

Directions:

1. In a medium bowl, combine all the ingredients.

MY TIPS:

TEMPEH HASH

Yields 2 to 4 servings

Most of my friends and family love the typical eggs-and-bacon breakfast, but this Sunday crowd-pleaser always has people going back for seconds. If you have an eggs-and-bacon crowd coming over for brunch, serve this up. They're sure to be impressed.

Ingredients:

1 tablespoon canola or vegetable oil (or 3 tablespoons water)

½ cup finely diced green or red bell pepper (about ½ bell pepper)

½ cup finely diced red, white, or yellow onion (about ½ medium onion)

1 teaspoon minced garlic (about 2 small cloves)

1 microwaved sweet potato (about 1 pound), diced (see page 238)

1 microwaved russet potato (about 1 pound), diced (see page 238)

1 batch Tempeh Bacon (see page 250)

Optional Additions:

Another ½–1 teaspoon minced garlic added in step 1

½ teaspoon ground cumin added in step 2

Directions:

1. In a large pan over medium-high heat, heat the oil (or water). Add the bell pepper, onion, and garlic and sauté for 5 minutes or until the bell pepper and onion are tender.
2. Add the potatoes and tempeh and stir.
3. Lower the heat to medium-low and cook for 10 minutes, stirring occasionally.
4. Serve immediately.

TESTERS' TIPS:

>> "If you don't have a microwave, dice the potatoes and put them in the oven at 400 degrees for 25 minutes." —Erica S. from Huntington Beach, CA

MY TIPS:

TROPICAL SMOOTHIE BOWL

Yields 1 to 2 servings

It took me a long time to jump on the smoothie bowl bandwagon, but my dear friend Michelle Cehn from the blog *World of Vegan* has got me hooked. Smoothie bowls provide texture and substance that make smoothies feel more like a proper breakfast. Plus, they're always a hit on Instagram!

Ingredients:

2 cups frozen mango chunks

½ cup frozen pineapple chunks

1 frozen banana

½–1 cup plant-based milk

2 tablespoons chopped nuts of your choice

¼ cup chopped fruit of your choice

Optional Toppings:

1 tablespoon flaxseed meal

1½ tablespoons coconut shreds

Directions:

1. Add the mango, pineapple, banana, and milk (1 cup makes it a thinner smoothie and ½ cup makes it thicker) to a blender and blend until smooth.

2. Pour the smoothie into a bowl and top with the nuts and fruit.

MY TIPS:

SALADS

*For the longest time, I refused to eat salads. In my
pre-plant-powered days, obviously, I avoided them. But even after
I took up the banner of veganism, I continued to shun leafy meals.
I didn't want to perpetuate the misconception that vegans only eat
salad. Now, I'm much more secure in my eating habits, and I've
come to appreciate how extremely tasty and filling a good salad can
be—not to mention that it's packed with nutrients.*

QUINOA SALAD

Yields 2 to 4 servings

Once you make the quinoa for this recipe, the possibilities for spicing it up are endless. You can add in any kinds of olives, chopped spinach or kale, garlic, finely chopped steamed carrots, and more.

Ingredients:

3 cups quinoa cooked in vegetable broth (see page 242)

½ cup chopped tomato

¾ cup diced cucumber (about ½ cucumber)

¾ cup diced red, white, or yellow onion (about 1 small onion)

¾ cup chopped green or kalamata olives

3 tablespoons lemon juice (about 1 small lemon)

Directions:

1. Cool the quinoa completely and transfer to a large bowl. Add the tomato, cucumber, onion, olives, and lemon juice. Mix well.

TESTERS' TIPS:

>>"I recommend adding some chopped-up Greek peperoncini in place of the olives because those are my absolute favorite to have in salads. They add a vinegar flavor like the olives do, but with some added spice." —Alex E.-P. from Sacramento, CA

>>"I added zucchini and lemon zest. Yummy! My husband, Scott, added lemon zest and cilantro." —Kathleen P. from Stockton, CA

MY TIPS:

MEXICAN-INSPIRED SALAD AND SWEET VINAIGRETTE

Yields 2 to 4 servings

This salad is one of my absolute favorites, and it's fair to say that it inspired me to jump on the salad bandwagon. I had a similar one at a restaurant in my hometown of Sacramento. Right after we paid the check, I raced home and immediately went to the kitchen to attempt to re-create it. If mangoes are in season, I highly recommend adding them. They bring an extra juicy, summertime flavor that complements the veggies well.

For the Salad:

3 cups chopped spinach

½ cup cilantro leaves

⅓ cup diced red onion

⅓ cup chopped raw pecans or walnuts

⅓ cup dried cranberries or raisins

For the Dressing:

2 tablespoons balsamic vinegar

½–1 tablespoon maple syrup or agave (depending on your sweetness preference)

1 tablespoon olive oil

Optional Additions:

1 fresh mango, diced, added in step 1

Directions:

1. In a large bowl, combine the spinach, cilantro, onion, pecans (or walnuts), and dried cranberries (or raisins).

2. In a separate small bowl, whisk together the balsamic vinegar, maple syrup (or agave), and olive oil.

3. Pour the dressing over the salad and toss together to thoroughly coat.

TESTERS' TIPS:

>> "Add some cooked quinoa or cooked wheat berries to make it a bit more substantial, if you want to have it as an entrée salad." —Lisa K. from New Orleans, LA

MY TIPS:

SLAW SALAD AND AVOCADO DRESSING

Yields 4 to 6 servings

My good friend and recipe tester Jenny Piccolo tried out this recipe, and she raved that it became one of her personal all-time, hall-of-fame favorites. After that kind of praise, I knew it had to be included in the book. Hope you love it as much as she does!

For the Salad:
2 cups thinly sliced red cabbage
1 cup grated carrots
¼ cup packed chopped cilantro

For the Dressing:
1 avocado, peeled and pitted
1 tablespoon lemon juice

¼ cup unsweetened plant-based milk
1–2 teaspoons minced garlic (depending on your garlic preference)
1–2 tablespoons Dijon mustard
½ tablespoon agave, brown sugar, or maple syrup
½ teaspoon salt

⅛ teaspoon freshly ground pepper

Optional Additions:
½ jalapeño, seeded and minced, added in step 2
2 tablespoons diced red onion added in step 2
1–2 teaspoons soy sauce added in step 2

Directions:
1. In a large bowl, mix the cabbage, carrots, and cilantro.
2. In a food processor or blender, blend together the avocado, lemon juice, milk, garlic, mustard, agave (or other sweetener), salt, and pepper until smooth.
3. Pour the dressing over the salad and toss well to coat.

TESTERS' TIPS:
>>"If you like a thinner dressing, add ¼ cup more plant-based milk." —Katie M. from Sacramento, CA

TLT SALAD

Yields 2 to 4 servings

If you're looking for a healthier, fresher take on the BLT, try this delicious TLT Salad. It's free of cholesterol and will leave you feeling a lot lighter.

Ingredients:

2 cups packed chopped romaine lettuce

¾ cup diced tomato

1 avocado, diced

1 batch Tempeh Bacon (see page 250), chopped

¾ cup Creamy Caesar Dressing (see page 83)

Directions:

1. In a large bowl, combine the lettuce, tomato, avocado, and Tempeh Bacon.
2. Top with the Caesar dressing and toss well to coat.

TONI'S TIPS:

>>Turn this salad into a sandwich using the same ingredients. Toast two slices of whole wheat bread, spread on some vegan mayo, add a slice of tomato, slices of Tempeh Bacon, a large lettuce leaf or two, and sliced avocado.

TESTERS' TIPS:

>>"This can also be made with tofu. Sub out the tempeh for tofu and follow the same instructions. It's just as tasty!" —Laura V. from Saint Paul, MN

MY TIPS:

BEAN AND CORN SALAD

Yields 4 to 6 servings

Michelle Cehn and I produced a mini-documentary called *7 Days*, featuring a young man who went from eating fast food daily to eating a mostly plant-based diet. He was the first person we ever coached. This is the first meal I taught him to make to reclaim his health. While working with this young man, we experienced his highs and lows of lifestyle change, and all three of us emerged on the other side as good friends. You can check it out at 7DaysDoc.com. This recipe is dedicated to that man, my friend Raul.

Ingredients:
1 (15-ounce) can pinto beans, drained and rinsed

1 (15-ounce) can black beans, drained and rinsed

1 (15-ounce) can chickpeas, drained and rinsed

1 (15-ounce) can unsalted corn, drained and rinsed

¾ cup diced tomato

¼ cup chopped cilantro

3–4 tablespoons lemon or lime juice (about 1 small lemon or lime)

Salt, to taste

Optional Additions:
1 avocado, diced, added in step 1

½ cup diced red onion (about ½ medium onion) added in step 1

½ teaspoon minced garlic (about 1 small clove) added in step 1

Directions:
1. In a large bowl, mix together all the ingredients. The salad can be served chilled or at room temperature.

TONI'S TIPS:

>>To make this a meal, serve it over a bed of brown rice. I also recommend adding it to the Loaded Sweet Potatoes recipe (see page 175).

>>If your canned beans and corn have salt, you don't have to add salt to the dish.

TESTERS' TIPS:

>>"I like salads with crunch and seasonings, so I recommend adding some matchstick-sized pieces of jicama or carrot, and maybe some cumin or chili powder. If serving over rice, definitely skip the crunchies, but I love this over lettuce!" —Susan M. from Kingsland, GA

MY TIPS:

CABBAGE SALAD AND PEANUT BUTTER VINAIGRETTE

Yields 2 to 4 servings

Make this recipe as is for a great starter salad, or top it with tofu and your favorite salad fixings for a full-on meal.

Ingredients:

3 tablespoons creamy peanut butter

2 tablespoons rice vinegar

2 tablespoons full-fat coconut milk

1 tablespoon soy sauce

½ tablespoon maple syrup, agave, or
   brown sugar

2 cups shredded red cabbage

1 cup shredded green or red cabbage

1 cup chopped unsalted roasted
   peanuts

Optional Additions:

½ teaspoon sesame oil added in step 1

½ cucumber, sliced, added in step 2

1 cup pressed and diced extra-firm tofu
   (see page 18) added in step 2

Directions:

1. In a medium bowl, whisk together the peanut butter, rice vinegar, coconut milk, soy sauce, and maple syrup (or other sweetener).
2. In a large bowl, combine the red and green cabbage and peanuts. Top with the dressing and stir to coat evenly.

TONI'S TIPS:

>>Water or any other plant-based milk can be used in place of coconut milk in a pinch.

CHICKPEA SALAD

Yields 4 to 6 servings

When I was younger, I ate *so* many tuna sandwiches. They were delicious and easy enough for a kid to make. All I had to do was open up a can of tuna, add some diced veggies and a dollop of mayo, and—boom—lunch was served. This recipe brings me back to those days, and the taste is surprisingly familiar. Thankfully, this salad features a cheaper, healthier, more sustainable, kinder protein. Plus, I think it's much tastier to boot.

Ingredients:

2 (15-ounce) cans chickpeas, drained and rinsed

3 tablespoons vegan mayonnaise

½ tablespoon classic mustard

¼ cup diced red onion

¼ cup diced celery (about 1 rib)

Salt and pepper, to taste

Optional Additions:

1–2 tablespoons diced dill pickles added in step 2

½ teaspoon kelp powder added in step 2

½ cup halved grape tomatoes added in step 2

1 cup shredded romaine lettuce added in step 2

Directions:

1. In a large bowl, mash the chickpeas with a potato masher or fork.
2. Add the mayonnaise, mustard, onion, celery, salt, and pepper, and mix together thoroughly.
3. Serve the salad on its own, wrap it in lettuce or pita, or scoop it up with crackers or chips.

TONI'S TIPS:

>> If you don't have vegan mayo, you can change up the flavors by adding more mustard and 1 tablespoon red wine vinegar.

>> To save time, you can pulse the chickpeas in a food processor for a couple of seconds instead of mashing them by hand.

MY TIPS:

LARB SALAD

Yields 4 servings

I grew up with many Hmong friends, who introduced me to the traditional version of this dish. I've since given it a healthy, plant-based makeover, and my version is crammed with flavor.

Ingredients:

1 teaspoon canola or vegetable oil

1 (14-ounce) block extra-firm tofu, pressed and crumbled (see page 18)

3 tablespoons lime juice (about 1½ limes), divided

2½ tablespoons minced cilantro

2 tablespoons soy sauce

1 green onion, sliced

½ tablespoon minced jalapeño

¼ cup thinly sliced red, white, or yellow onion

2 tablespoons minced mint

8 iceberg or romaine lettuce leaves

Directions:

1. Heat the oil in a saucepan over medium heat. Add the tofu and 1 tablespoon of the lime juice, and sauté for 4 to 5 minutes or until the tofu is light brown.

2. Place the tofu in a medium bowl and combine with the remaining 2 tablespoons lime juice, cilantro, soy sauce, green onion, jalapeño, onion, and mint. Mix well.

3. Serve in the lettuce leaves.

MY TIPS:

KALE SALAD AND CREAMY CAESAR DRESSING

Yields 4 to 6 servings

The original version of this recipe came from the kitchen of my friend Grace Kuhn. Through various tweaks of my own and my recipe testers, it's morphed into this flavorful goodness of a kale salad. Grace has been a huge supporter of Plant-Based on a Budget since the beginning and has even contributed meal plans to the site, which have helped thousands of people. Thanks, G!

Ingredients:

½ cup cubed firm tofu

½ cup olive oil

2 cloves garlic

2½ tablespoons lemon juice

2 tablespoons white vinegar

2 tablespoons Dijon mustard

2 tablespoons capers

Salt and pepper, to taste

4 cups packed chopped kale

Optional Toppings:

Croutons (see page 233)

½ cup halved grape or cherry tomatoes

1 batch Tempeh Bacon, chopped (see page 250)

Directions:

1. In a blender or food processor, blend the tofu, olive oil, garlic, lemon juice, vinegar, and mustard until thoroughly combined.

2. Add the capers, salt, and pepper, and stir together with a spoon.

3. Place the kale in a bowl, top with the creamy tofu dressing, and thoroughly massage the dressing into the kale. Add any optional toppings.

TONI'S TIPS:

>> Massaging the kale with the dressing will make it softer to chew and easier to digest. It'll also reduce the bitterness.

MY TIPS:

BASIC TABLE SALAD

Yields 2 to 4 servings

As much as I love the fancier salads in this chapter, this is the one that usually tops my dining room table. It's simple, all-purpose, and versatile and pairs great with my Sweet Vinaigrette (see page 66).

Ingredients:

1 head romaine lettuce or spinach, coarsely chopped

½ cup sliced red, white, or yellow onion (about ½ medium onion)

½–1 cucumber, cut in quarters

1 cup halved cherry or grape tomatoes

⅔ cup Sweet Vinaigrette (see page 66) or your favorite dressing

Optional Additions:

1 cup pressed and diced extra-firm tofu (see page 18) added in step 1

1 avocado, diced, added in step 1

Sprinkle of nutritional yeast, added in step 1

Sunflower or pumpkin seeds, added in step 1

Directions:

1. In a large bowl, combine the lettuce, onion, cucumber, and tomatoes.
2. Top with the dressing and toss to coat.

MY TIPS:

_____

_____

_____

_____

STIC'S DATE NITE POWER SNACK

Yields 2 servings

Back when I first started my blog, I reached out to one of my favorite rappers, Stic of Dead Prez, to see if he'd be interested in collaborating with me in some way. He's been someone I've admired for *years*. I didn't think for one second that he'd respond, but he came back to me with this beautifully written article called "7 Ways to Eat Good on a Hood Budget" that he said I could post to my blog. It ended up going viral, and even better, we became friends. I'm so grateful for his contributions to my site and this book. Here's his quick and delicious favorite snack recipe. I'll let him describe it in his own words:

This delicious nutrient-dense family favorite is fresh, crispy, nutty, sweet, satisfying, filling, inexpensive, and super simple and quick to make.

I personally like it best with raisins, but wifey likes it with medjool dates, hence the name "date nite." Almost unfailingly, every night she has her ritual of hot herbal tea and her "date nite" snack plate to relax and wind down from the day. It's a great go-to snack when you want something tasty, quick, and satisfying without having to cook or reach for junk food.

Ingredients:
2 small apples, sliced

½ cup peanut butter (creamy or chunky)

¼ cup raisins, or 2–3 dates, pitted and halved

Optional Toppings:
⅛ cup coconut flakes

Pinch of cinnamon

Directions:
1. Place the apple slices peel down on a plate. Smear the peanut butter on top of each slice, using 1 to 2 tablespoons for each.
2. Sprinkle the raisins (or dates) over the peanut butter side and enjoy.
3. If you're feeling gourmet fancy, sprinkle with the optional toppings.

MY TIPS:

NACHO CHEESE

Yields 3 cups

This recipe made its debut appearance in my first book, *The Super Easy Vegan Slow Cooker Cookbook*. Since then, I've tweaked the measurements. Consider this the improved 2.0 version.

Ingredients:

2 cups peeled and diced russet potatoes

1 cup sliced carrots

½ cup water

1 tablespoon lemon juice

½ cup nutritional yeast

1 teaspoon onion powder

1 teaspoon garlic powder

½ teaspoon salt

Optional Additions:

¼ cup salsa added in step 2

Directions:

1. Fill a large pot with water and add the potatoes and carrots. Over medium-high heat, bring the water to a boil and keep cooking for 10 minutes or until the veggies are soft. Remove from the heat and drain the water.

2. In a blender, blend the boiled potatoes, carrots, water, lemon juice, nutritional yeast, onion powder, garlic powder, and salt until completely smooth.

TONI'S TIPS:

>>With several other recipes in this book, it won't hurt to add a bit more or less of a veggie. But here, I recommend measuring out the potato and carrot exactly rather than eyeballing their amounts. I found that adding more or less of each of these changes the consistency and makes the mixture seem less cheesy.

TESTERS' TIPS:

>>"The day after I made this, I added a little over half of my Nacho Cheese to about 8 ounces macaroni noodles. It made a really nice and easy mac and cheese! Another day, I also used it as a topping on a baked potato, which was also delicious!"
—Melanie S. from Warsaw, NY

TOMATILLO SALSA

Yields 2½ cups

This is another summertime staple for me. I love it as a snack with chips, but you can also add this to your meals: it goes perfectly with Chilaquiles (see page 45) or Totchos (see page 190).

Ingredients:

8 small tomatillos (about 1 pound)

½ white onion, cut in half

1½ teaspoons minced garlic (about 3 small cloves)

1 jalapeño, halved and seeded

⅓ cup packed chopped cilantro

1 (4-ounce) can chopped mild green chili peppers

Optional Additions:

½ tablespoon ground cumin added in step 5

Salt and pepper, to taste, added in step 5

Seeds from jalapeño (for spice) added in step 5

Directions:

1. Preheat the broiler. Line a large baking sheet with aluminum foil.
2. Prep the tomatillos: remove their husks, wash them, and cut them in half.
3. Place the tomatillos and onion face down on the prepared baking sheet. Add the garlic and jalapeño to the baking sheet.
4. Broil for 5 to 7 minutes or until everything is evenly charred.
5. In a blender or food processor, pulse the charred ingredients, cilantro, and chili peppers until the salsa is smooth.

TONI'S TIPS:

>>After removing the husks from the tomatillos, they'll feel a little sticky. Give them a good wash before broiling.

TESTERS' TIPS:

>>"Adding this to guacamole is very tasty if you're looking for a variation." —Michelle R. from Saint Paul, MN

MY TIPS:

PEANUT BUTTER BALLS

Yields 12 balls

I originally came up with this recipe for the snack e-book on PlantBasedMealPlan .com, and it was such a huge hit that I wanted to make sure it was included here. What makes it so popular? Apart from being capital-*D* delicious, it's also a recipe with only three ingredients. That's my favorite kind! Once you're done prepping these, toss them into an airtight container or plastic bag and store them in the refrigerator for up to 5 days. They're great to keep on hand whenever you need a snack.

Ingredients:

1 cup old-fashioned
  rolled oats
½ cup creamy peanut
  butter
¼ cup raisins

Optional Additions:

¼ cup vegan semisweet
  mini chocolate chips
  added in step 1
¼ cup coconut shreds
  added in step 1
¼ cup chopped nuts
  added in step 1

Directions:

1. Add all the ingredients to a large bowl. Using your hands, mix together thoroughly.
2. Roll the mixture into small balls with your hands, making each about the size of a tablespoon. Place the balls on a baking sheet.
3. Put the baking sheet into the freezer for 30 minutes.
4. Remove from the freezer and eat immediately, or store in an airtight container or plastic bag in your refrigerator for up to 5 days.

TONI'S TIPS:

>> These make a great kid-friendly cooking project. You can invite the whole family to join in the fun. Set up a workstation that has the three main ingredients, and maybe a second station with optional additions like mini chocolate chips, coconut shreds, or chopped nuts. Just make sure to add extra peanut butter if you're adding extra ingredients.

>> For the peanut butter, be sure to use one that's well blended, not the kind where the oil separates out.

>>"If the balls are not quite sticking together when you're rolling them, try squeezing the mix tightly in your hand and then forming it into balls." —Laura V. from Saint Paul, MN

>>"I pressed all the dough into my Pyrex bread pan, stuck that in the freezer, and cut twelve bars that way. It made the process even quicker." —Toube B. from Chico, CA

MY TIPS:

ONE-POT MEALS

Although this book has a strong emphasis on saving money, I'm also a huge booster of saving time—especially when it comes to cooking and cleaning. That's why I was determined to write a one-pot meals chapter. Don't waste time washing a bunch of dishes on weeknights—instead, throw one of these simple yet flavorful meals together. Nearly every recipe in this chapter can be made in a pressure cooker, too.

BLACK BEAN SOUP

Yields 6 to 8 servings

This recipe can go one of two ways: If you want to save money but you have time to spare, buy beans in bulk and make this protein-packed recipe even more inexpensive (see page 228 for cooking instructions). If you want to save on time, buy canned beans and your prep time is only minutes.

Ingredients:

1 tablespoon canola or vegetable oil (or 3 tablespoons water)

¾ cup diced red, white, or yellow onion (about 1 small onion)

1 teaspoon minced garlic (about 2 small cloves)

½ jalapeño, seeded and minced

1 tablespoon ground cumin

1 teaspoon dried oregano

1 bay leaf

4½ cups water and 2 vegetable bouillon cubes, or 4½ cups vegetable broth

6 (15-ounce) cans black beans, drained and rinsed

Salt, to taste

Optional Additions:

1 cup corn kernels added after step 5

Optional Toppings:

Minced cilantro

Diced red onion

Hot sauce

Squeeze of lime juice

Directions:

1. In a large pot over medium-high heat, heat the oil (or water). Add the onion, garlic, and jalapeño and sauté for 5 minutes or until the onion is tender and translucent.
2. Add the cumin, oregano, and bay leaf and cook for 2 more minutes.
3. Add the water and bouillon cubes (or broth), black beans, and salt and reduce the heat to medium. Cook for 15 minutes.
4. Remove from the heat and take out the bay leaf.
5. Using an immersion blender (or a regular blender, working in batches), purée the soup until it is the desired consistency.

TONI'S TIPS:

>> This works great in the pressure cooker. Throw everything into the pressure cooker and cook on high pressure for 5 minutes. Then continue to step 5.

TESTERS' TIPS:

>> "If you want some texture, blend just two-thirds of the soup to leave in some whole black beans." —Caryn G. from Arlington, VA

MY TIPS:

BROCCOLI POTATO SOUP

Yields 6 to 8 servings

Turn a bag of potatoes into a comforting and delicious meal with this Broccoli Potato Soup.

Ingredients:

½ tablespoon canola or vegetable oil (or 3 tablespoons water)

1 cup diced red, white, or yellow onion (about 1 medium onion)

1 teaspoon minced garlic (about 2 small cloves)

5 cups water and 2½ vegetable bouillon cubes, or 5 cups vegetable broth

6 cups chopped russet or red potatoes (about 8 small potatoes)

1 (10-ounce) bag frozen broccoli or 3 crowns of fresh broccoli, chopped

Juice of 1 small lemon

Pinch of pepper

Optional Additions:

1 (15-ounce) can chickpeas, drained and rinsed, added in step 2

Optional Toppings:

Red chili flakes

Directions:

1. In a medium pan over medium-low heat, heat the oil (or water). Add the onion and garlic and sauté for 5 minutes or until the onion becomes tender and translucent.
2. Add the water and bouillon cubes (or broth), potatoes, broccoli, lemon juice, and pepper.
3. Bring to a boil.
4. Boil until the potatoes are cooked all the way through, 10 to 15 minutes.
5. Remove from the heat. Purée half of the soup using an immersion blender (or with a regular blender, working in batches). Return the puréed soup to the pot and combine with the remaining soup.

TONI'S TIPS:

>>This works great in the pressure cooker. Throw everything into the pressure cooker and cook on high pressure for 5 minutes. Then continue to step 4.

>>Replace the lemon juice with ½ cup nutritional yeast.

TESTERS' TIPS:

>>"Adding celery in step 1 will give a nice complexity to the flavor." —Anna W. from Davis, CA

CARROT GINGER SOUP

Yields 4 to 6 servings

This thick and creamy soup is filling and delicious. Serve it as a side with a big salad or as the main dish with a hunk of homemade bread.

Ingredients:

1 tablespoon canola or vegetable oil (or 3 tablespoons water)

1 cup diced red, white, or yellow onion (about 1 medium onion)

1 teaspoon minced garlic (about 2 small cloves)

2 tablespoons minced ginger (about 1½-inch piece)

3 cups chopped carrots (about 6 large carrots)

2 cups chopped russet potatoes (about 1 large potato)

4 cups water and 2 vegetable bouillon cubes, or 4 cups vegetable broth

Salt and pepper, to taste

Optional Additions:

½ jalapeño (for spice), seeded and minced, added in step 2

½ cup full-fat coconut milk added in step 4

¼ cup nutritional yeast added in step 4

1 teaspoon cayenne pepper (for spice) added in step 4

Directions:

1. In a large pot, heat the oil (or water) over medium-high heat.
2. Add the onion, garlic, and ginger and sauté for 2 to 3 minutes or until the onion becomes translucent and tender.
3. Add the carrots, potatoes, and water and bouillon cubes (or broth), and cook for 20 minutes or until the carrots and potatoes are tender.
4. Remove from the heat. Purée the soup using an immersion blender (or with a regular blender, working in batches). Add salt and pepper.

TONI'S TIPS:

>>This works great in the pressure cooker. Throw everything but the oil into the pressure cooker and cook on high pressure for 6 minutes. If you're using coconut milk, stir that in after the soup is finished cooking.

COCONUT CURRY SOUP

Yields 4 to 6 servings

A couple of years ago, my dear friend Gretchen shared a similar curry soup recipe with me. Over the years, I've tweaked it following my own tips (like the kind you'll find throughout the book), and it's evolved into a mainstay. I love that every ingredient is interchangeable. You can replace the rice with couscous or quinoa, throw in whatever veggies you've got on hand, and mix up the spice level to suit your palate. Below is my favorite version.

Ingredients:

1 tablespoon canola or vegetable oil (or 3 tablespoons water)

¾ cup diced red, white, or yellow onion (about 1 small onion)

1½ teaspoons minced garlic (about 3 small cloves)

1 cup diced green or red bell pepper (about 1 medium bell pepper)

1 (14.5-ounce) can diced tomatoes with their juices

1 (15-ounce) can chickpeas, drained and rinsed

4 cups water and 2 vegetable bouillon cubes, or 4 cups vegetable broth

1½ teaspoons ground cumin

2½ teaspoons curry powder

1 (13.5-ounce) can full-fat coconut milk

½ cup cooked brown rice (see page 226)

Salt and pepper, to taste

Optional Toppings:

Red chili flakes

Minced cilantro

Directions:

1. In a large pot, heat the oil (or water) over medium heat.
2. Add the onion, garlic, and bell pepper. Cook, stirring occasionally, for 5 minutes or until the veggies are tender.
3. Add the tomatoes, chickpeas, water and bouillon cubes (or broth), cumin, and curry powder. Bring to a boil. Reduce the heat to low and simmer gently, stirring occasionally, for 10 minutes.
4. Add the coconut milk and brown rice and cook for 5 minutes, stirring occasionally.
5. Add salt and pepper.

>>This works great in the pressure cooker. Throw everything but the coconut milk and rice (and skip the oil) into the pressure cooker and cook on high pressure for 4 minutes. Then continue to step 4.

TESTERS' TIPS:

>>"Try adding kale for some color and texture. I also recommend adding sliced mushrooms." —Cathy B. from Columbia, MD

MY TIPS:

FOUR-BEAN CHILI

Yields 4 to 6 servings

A little backstory for this recipe: I've known my best friend, Candice, for over half of my life, and she never remembers my birthday. One year, Candice invited me over and made me a fabulous chili dinner and gave me flowers. I thought, "Wow! She is going above and beyond getting me a card for Valentine's Day." But when I was leaving, she gave me a hug and called out, "Happy birthday!" Hey, at least she got the month right. Now, I always think of her when I make this Four-Bean Chili, which is inspired by the (un)birthday meal she made me that night.

Ingredients:

1 tablespoon canola or vegetable oil (or 3 tablespoons water)

1 cup diced red, white, or yellow onion (about 1 medium onion)

1 teaspoon minced garlic (about 2 small cloves)

¾ cup diced green or red bell pepper (about 1 small bell pepper)

½ cup diced zucchini

1 (14.5-ounce) can diced tomatoes with their juices

1 (15-ounce) can black beans, drained and rinsed

1 (15-ounce) can pinto beans, drained and rinsed

1 (15-ounce) can kidney beans, drained and rinsed

2 (15-ounce) cans chickpeas, drained and rinsed

3 tablespoons ground cumin

2 teaspoons chili powder

1 (6-ounce) can tomato paste

½ cup water

Salt, to taste

Optional Additions:

½−1 teaspoon cayenne pepper, red chili flakes, or minced jalapeño added in step 3

Optional Toppings:

Chopped cilantro

Sliced avocado

Minced onion

Squeeze of lime juice

Directions:

1. In a large pot over medium-high heat, heat the oil (or water).
2. Add the onion, garlic, and bell pepper and sauté until the veggies are tender and the onion is translucent.
3. Add the zucchini, tomatoes, beans, chickpeas, cumin, chili powder, tomato paste, water, and salt. Mix together.
4. Lower the heat to medium-low and cook for 15 minutes, stirring occasionally.
5. Serve and top with optional toppings.

TONI'S TIPS:

>>This works great in the pressure cooker. Throw everything into the pressure cooker and cook on high pressure for 5 minutes. Then continue to step 5.

>>This is a great recipe if you want to use what you have on hand. If you want it to be a two-bean chili because you have two cans of black beans and two cans of pinto (or whatever kind), that's fine. If you want to throw in extra veggies, that's fine, too.

TESTERS' TIPS:

>>"This tastes even better on the second day." —Isabelle C. from Los Altos, CA

MY TIPS:

MY TIPS:

GINGER BUTTERNUT SQUASH SOUP

Yields 6 to 8 servings

During the winter months, I like doubling this soup and freezing it for nights when I'm feeling too tired to cook. It's like a cozy sweater in soup form.

Ingredients:

1 tablespoon canola or vegetable oil (or 3 tablespoons water)

½ cup diced red, white, or yellow onion (about ½ medium onion)

1 teaspoon minced garlic (about 2 small cloves)

2 tablespoons minced ginger (about 1½-inch piece)

6 cups frozen or roasted cubed butternut squash (about 3 small squashes) (see page 238)

½ cup full-fat coconut milk

4 cups water and 2 vegetable bouillon cubes, or 4 cups vegetable broth

1 tablespoon curry powder

¼ teaspoon cayenne pepper

Salt and pepper, to taste

Optional Additions:

½ jalapeño, seeded and minced, added in step 2

1 (15-ounce) can pinto beans, drained and rinsed, added in step 2

Directions:

1. In a large pot over medium-high heat, heat the oil (or water). Add the onion, garlic, and ginger and sauté for 4 minutes or until the onion is tender and translucent.
2. Add the butternut squash, coconut milk, water and bouillon cubes (or broth), curry powder, and cayenne pepper.
3. Turn the heat down to medium-low and cook for 20 minutes.
4. Add salt and pepper.

TONI'S TIPS:

>>This works great in the pressure cooker. Throw everything except the oil in the pressure cooker and cook on high pressure for 5 minutes. Then continue to step 4.

MISO SPLIT PEA SOUP

Yields 6 to 8 servings

This is another recipe that was such a huge hit in *The Super Easy Vegan Slow Cooker Cookbook* that I had to adapt it for the stovetop and include it in this book.

Ingredients:

1 tablespoon canola or vegetable oil (or 3 tablespoons water)

1 cup diced red, white, or yellow onion (about 1 medium onion)

1 teaspoon minced garlic (about 2 small cloves)

1 cup diced carrot (about 1 large carrot)

¾ cup diced celery (about 2 ribs)

2 batches cooked green split peas (see page 232)

6 cups water and 3 vegetable bouillon cubes, or 6 cups vegetable broth

2 tablespoons yellow or white miso

1 bay leaf

Salt and pepper, to taste

Optional Additions:

½ teaspoon liquid smoke added in step 3

½ cup nutritional yeast added in step 3

Directions:

1. In a large pot over medium-high heat, heat the oil (or water).
2. Add the onion, garlic, carrot, and celery and sauté for 3 to 4 minutes.
3. Add the split peas, water and bouillon cubes (or broth), miso, and bay leaf. Cook for 15 minutes or until the veggies are tender.
4. Remove from the heat. Add salt and pepper.

TONI'S TIPS:

>>For regular split pea soup, just leave out the miso in step 3.

>>The longer you let your split peas cook, the more they split. If you like them to be totally creamy, let them cook longer.

>>If you're batch cooking in order to make leftovers, keep in mind that this soup will thicken over time. You can either thin it out by adding water or keep it thick and serve it over brown rice. (For a brown rice recipe, see page 226.)

>>This works great in the pressure cooker. Throw everything into the pressure cooker and cook on high pressure for 3 minutes. Then continue to step 4.

MY TIPS:

MEXICAN-INSPIRED SOUP

Yields 4 to 6 servings

Growing up in a Mexican family, I loved the special occasions my family served us menudo. When I became vegan, I thought I'd really miss it. Then I realized that when I used to eat it back in my pre-vegan days, I'd always pick out the tripe and eat the broth and hominy. Here's my replacement to fulfill my need for that tasty, tasty soup.

Ingredients:

1 tablespoon canola or vegetable oil (or 3 tablespoons water)

1½ teaspoons minced garlic (about 3 small cloves)

1 cup diced red, white, or yellow onion (about 1 medium onion)

2 carrots, thinly sliced

2 ribs celery, thinly sliced

2 cups chopped frozen or fresh broccoli

1 (15.5-ounce) can hominy, drained

1 tablespoon lime juice (about ½ lime)

4 cups water and 2 vegetable bouillon cubes, or 4 cups vegetable broth

¼ cup minced cilantro

Salt and pepper, to taste

Directions:

1. In a large pot over medium-high heat, heat the oil (or water).
2. Add the garlic and onion and sauté until the onion becomes tender and translucent.
3. Add the carrots, celery, broccoli, hominy, and lime juice.
4. Pour in the water and bouillon cubes (or broth). Bring to a boil, then reduce the heat and simmer for 20 minutes.
5. Stir in the cilantro and add salt and pepper.

TONI'S TIPS:

>>Hominy is found in the Mexican foods aisle of grocery stores.

>>This works great in the pressure cooker. Throw everything except the oil in the pressure cooker and cook on high pressure for 3 minutes. Then continue to step 5.

TESTERS' TIPS:

>>"I love this soup and made it my own by adding 1 teaspoon cumin and using zucchini instead of broccoli." —Lisa O. from Sacramento, CA

FANCY INSTANT RAMEN SOUP

Yields 2 to 4 servings

Instant ramen was the first thing I ever learned to cook. I would constantly beg my grandma to make it for me. Eventually, to give herself a break, she taught me how to make it when I was five or six years old. I've been making it ever since. Here's how I dress it up.

Ingredients:

6 cups water

½ cup chopped frozen broccoli

½ cup frozen mixed vegetables

½ teaspoon minced garlic (about 1 small clove)

3 (3-ounce) packages instant ramen noodles

Optional Additions:

¼ cup sautéed diced onion added in step 2

¼ teaspoon red chili flakes added after step 3

1 cup pressed and diced extra-firm tofu added after step 3 (see page 18)

Freshly ground pepper, to taste, added in step 4

Directions:

1. In a large pot over high heat, bring the water to a boil.
2. Add the broccoli, mixed vegetables, and garlic. Boil for 5 minutes.
3. Stir in the ramen noodles and cook the noodles according to the directions on the package, but use only two of the three seasoning packets.
4. Remove from the heat. Serve immediately.

TONI'S TIPS:

>>Remember to look for plant-based ramen. The "soy sauce" version from Nissin's Top Ramen is vegan. (The package is blue and says "vegetarian" on it.) There are also plenty of natural instant ramen brands that are fantastic and cheap.

MY TIPS:

MINESTRONE SOUP

Yields 6 to 8 servings

This is it. The perfect soup for a rainy day. Pour yourself a bowl of this, grab your favorite cozy blanket, and put on your favorite episode of *Gilmore Girls*. You're in for a treat.

Ingredients:

1 tablespoon canola or vegetable oil (or 3 tablespoons water)

½ cup diced red, white, or yellow onion (about ½ medium onion)

1 teaspoon minced garlic (about 2 small cloves)

2 carrots, thinly sliced

2 ribs celery, thinly sliced

1 (14.5-ounce) can diced tomatoes with their juices

5 cups water and 2½ vegetable bouillon cubes, or 5 cups vegetable broth

2 (15-ounce) cans kidney beans, drained and rinsed

1 teaspoon dried oregano

1 teaspoon ground cumin

1½ cups shaped pasta (bowties, rigatoni, penne, etc.)

Salt and pepper, to taste

Optional Additions:

2 bay leaves added in step 3

2 cups chopped kale or spinach added in step 3

2 medium russet or red potatoes, chopped, added in step 3

1 cup fresh or frozen chopped broccoli added in step 3

1 cup fresh or frozen green beans added in step 3

Directions:

1. In a large pot over medium-high heat, heat the oil (or water).
2. Add the onion, garlic, carrots, and celery. Sauté for 3 minutes or until the onion is tender and translucent.
3. Add the tomatoes, water and bouillon cubes (or broth), beans, oregano, and cumin, and cook for 5 minutes.
4. Add the pasta and cook for the amount of time suggested on the package.
5. Remove from the heat. Add salt and pepper.

>>This works great in the pressure cooker. Throw everything except the pasta and oil in the pressure cooker and cook on high pressure for 5 minutes. Then continue to step 4.

TESTERS' TIPS:

>>"A tip if you want to freeze the soup—leave the pasta out. It will get mushy and fall apart in the freezer. But if you skip the pasta now, you can always cook it separately later and add it to the soup after you've defrosted it." —Lisa K. from New Orleans, LA

MY TIPS:

GUMBO

Yields 6 to 8 servings

This gumbo always reminds me of my first trip to New Orleans. I traveled with my friend Drea, and we had the absolute best time swing dancing to live jazz bands, wearing pretty vintage-inspired dresses, and visiting nearly every vegan-friendly restaurant in search of traditional NOLA food. If you want a more authentic taste, I recommend adding the vegan sausage. Lightlife's Gimme Lean has been my go-to sausage for the past ten years.

Ingredients:
1 tablespoon canola or vegetable oil (or
    3 tablespoons water)
½ cup diced red, white, or yellow onion
    (about ½ medium onion)
1 teaspoon garlic (about 2 small cloves)
¾ cup sliced celery (about 2 ribs)
½ jalapeño, seeded and minced
1 cup chopped green or red bell pepper
    (about 1 medium bell pepper)
1 cup chopped frozen or fresh okra
1 (14.5-ounce) can fire-roasted
    tomatoes with their juices

2 (15-ounce) cans black beans, drained
    and rinsed
1–3 teaspoons Cajun seasoning
    (depending on your spiciness
    preference)
4 cups water and 2 vegetable bouill
    cubes, or 4 cups vegetable broth
Salt and pepper, to taste

Optional Additions:
Pan-fried store-bought vegan sausage
    added after step 3.

Directions:
1. In a large pot over medium-high heat, heat the oil (or water).
2. Add the onion, garlic, celery, jalapeño, bell pepper, and okra and cook for 3 minutes, stirring occasionally.
3. Add the tomatoes, beans, Cajun seasoning, and water and bouillon cubes (or broth), and cook for 20 minutes.
4. Add salt and pepper.

>>This works great in the pressure cooker. Throw everything into the pressure cooker and cook on high pressure for 5 minutes. Then continue to step 4.

MY TIPS:

SWEET POTATO CHILI

Yields 4 to 6 servings

With its vivid orange color, this recipe always reminds me of autumn. When the leaves start falling, this chili becomes one of my favorite pressure cooker recipes.

Ingredients:
½ tablespoon canola or vegetable oil (or 1½ tablespoons water)

½ cup diced red, white, or yellow onion (about ½ medium onion)

1 teaspoon minced garlic (about 2 small cloves)

1 (14.5-ounce) can diced tomatoes with their juices

2 tablespoons ground cumin

1 tablespoon chili powder

½ teaspoon cayenne pepper

½–1 teaspoon salt

2 microwaved sweet potatoes, diced (see page 238)

3 (15-ounce) cans black, kidney, or pinto beans, drained and rinsed

Optional Additions:
¼–½ teaspoon cinnamon added in step 3

1 cup cooked quinoa (see page 224) added in step 3

Directions:
1. In a large pot over medium-high heat, heat the oil (or water).
2. Add the onion and garlic and sauté for 3 minutes or until the onion is tender and translucent.
3. Add the tomatoes, cumin, chili powder, cayenne pepper, and salt. Stir in the sweet potato and beans.
4. Reduce the heat to medium-low and cook for 15 minutes, stirring occasionally.

TONI'S TIPS:
>>This works great in the pressure cooker. Throw everything into the pressure cooker and cook on high pressure for 5 minutes.

TOFU NOODLE SOUP

Yields 6 to 8 servings

When I was young, my family would always keep our home stocked with Campbell's Chicken Noodle Soup. Now I've leveled up to this plant-based version.

Ingredients:

½ tablespoon canola or vegetable oil (or 3 tablespoons water)

½ cup diced red, white, or yellow onion (about ½ medium onion)

2 ribs celery, thinly sliced

2 carrots, thinly sliced

1 teaspoon minced garlic (about 2 small cloves)

6 cups water and 3 vegetable bouillon cubes, or 6 cups vegetable broth

1 (14-ounce) block extra-firm tofu, pressed and cut into ½-inch cubes (see page 18)

6 ounces pasta (rice noodles, udon, or shaped pasta)

Salt and pepper, to taste

Optional Additions:

1 cup fresh or frozen chopped broccoli added in step 2

½ cup thinly sliced zucchini added in step 2

Directions:

1. In a large pot over medium-high heat, heat the oil (or water).
2. Add the onion, celery, carrots, and garlic and sauté, stirring occasionally, for 5 minutes or until the onion is tender and translucent.
3. Add the water and bouillon cubes (or broth) and tofu and cook for another 5 minutes.
4. Add the noodles and cook for the amount of time suggested on the package.
5. Remove from the heat and sprinkle with salt and pepper.

TONI'S TIPS:

>>This works great in the pressure cooker. Throw everything into the pressure cooker except the noodles and oil and cook on high pressure for 4 minutes. Then continue to step 4.

SUPPER STAPLES

I believe dinner is extremely important. It's the time you literally break bread together and share your day with your family. In my home, I light a candle when dinner is served, and when the candle is lit, no one is allowed to fuss around with their technology (cell phones, computers, TV, and other devices are all switched off). And because I know how valuable this meal is, and because I too was once skeptical of vegan entrées, I have picked my most loved recipes for this chapter. It is my hope that many loving conversations happen over these meals and that they help your family embrace healthier, plant-based eating.

SWEET POTATO TACOS

Yields 2 servings

Back when I was a vegetarian, my friend Michelle Salemi made me some fabulous sweet potato quesadillas. Since I no longer eat dairy, I've turned her filling into a simple way to up my burrito and taco game. I serve it with a can of drained pinto or black beans, sliced avocado, and chopped tomatoes. If you want to be fancy, you can also throw on some vegan cheese shreds.

Ingredients:
½ tablespoon canola or vegetable oil
(or 3 tablespoons water)
¾ cup diced red, white, or yellow onion
(about 1 small onion)
1½ teaspoons minced garlic (about
3 small cloves)
4 cups finely diced or grated sweet
potatoes (about 2 sweet potatoes)
2 tablespoons water
1½ teaspoons chili powder
1½ tablespoons ground cumin
¼ teaspoon salt
Pepper, to taste
4 whole wheat or corn tortillas

Optional Additions:
¼ cup nutritional yeast and 2
tablespoons water added in step 3
¼ teaspoon cayenne pepper added in
step 3

Optional Toppings:
Sliced avocado
Minced cilantro
Shredded lettuce
Diced onion
Halved cherry tomatoes
Salsa
Vegan sour cream

Directions:
1. In a large pan over medium-high heat, heat the oil (or water).
2. Add the onion and garlic and sauté for 3 minutes or until the onion is tender and translucent.
3. Add the sweet potatoes, water, chili powder, cumin, salt, and pepper, and lower the heat to medium.
4. Cook for about 10 minutes, stirring frequently to avoid sticking. Remove from the heat.

5. Add one-quarter of the filling to each tortilla and top with any of the optional toppings you're using.

TONI'S TIPS:

>>If your potatoes are looking too dry toward the end of the 10-minute cooking time, you can add 1 tablespoon water.

TESTERS' TIPS:

>>"Toast the tortillas on the stove or in a pan before turning them into tacos. It makes a world of difference." —Logan J. from Sacramento, CA

MY TIPS:

MY TIPS:

TOFU WITH PEANUT SAUCE

Yields 2 servings

In the summer, when it's over 100 degrees here in Sacramento, the last thing I want to do is turn on the stove. That's when I reach for this recipe. I throw this sauce in a bowl and whip it together in minutes. If you want to add veggies, it's easy to micro-wave some frozen broccoli or mixed vegetables to add a nutritional boost. (You can, of course, use fresh steamed produce, too.) And if you want to make the dish heart-ier, you can serve it over brown rice or rice noodles.

Ingredients:

½ cup creamy peanut butter

2 tablespoons soy sauce

1 tablespoon lime juice (about ½ lime)

1 teaspoon minced garlic (about 2 small cloves)

⅓ cup water

¼ teaspoon red chili flakes

1 (14-ounce) block extra-firm tofu, pressed and cut into ½-inch cubes (see page 18)

Optional Toppings:

1 teaspoon sesame oil

½ teaspoon grated ginger

1 teaspoon hot sauce

¼ cup chopped unsalted roasted peanuts

Directions:

1. In a large bowl, mix together the peanut butter, soy sauce, lime juice, garlic, water, and red chili flakes until smooth and creamy.

2. Add the tofu to the peanut sauce and toss well until coated.

TONI'S TIPS:

>>You can easily make this gluten-free by swapping out the soy sauce for tamari.

>>If you want it to be creamier, add water one table-spoon at a time until desired consistency is achieved.

TESTERS' TIPS:

>>"Tastes great with fried tofu, too!" —Erica S. from Huntington Beach, CA

LENTIL TACOS

Yields 4 to 6 servings

My friend Terrence introduced me to the wonderful concept of lentil tacos about six years ago, and they've been in my dinner rotation ever since. (You can check out his less simplified version at PlantBasedonaBudget.com.)

Ingredients:

1 tablespoon canola or vegetable oil (or 3 tablespoons water)

½ cup diced red, white, or yellow onion (about ½ medium onion)

1 teaspoon minced garlic (about 2 small cloves)

1 cup uncooked lentils, rinsed

1½ tablespoons store-bought taco seasoning

1 cup water and 1 vegetable bouillon cube, or 1 cup vegetable broth

6 corn tortillas

Optional Toppings:

Dollop of vegan sour cream

Sliced avocado

Diced tomatoes

Shredded lettuce

½ cup salsa

Squeeze of lime juice

Directions:

1. In a medium pan or pot (with a lid) over medium-high heat, heat the oil (or water).
2. Add the onion and garlic and sauté for 3 minutes or until the onion is tender and translucent.
3. Add the lentils, taco seasoning, and water and bouillon cube (or broth). Bring to a boil, cover, and reduce the heat to low.
4. Simmer for 25 to 30 minutes.
5. Remove from the heat and scoop the lentils into the tortillas. Serve immediately.

TONI'S TIPS:

>>If you don't have taco seasoning, you can make your own by adding 1 tablespoon cumin and 1 teaspoon chili powder. You can also add a pinch of cayenne pepper if you have it.

AVOCADO SUNFLOWER SEED PESTO PASTA

Yields 2 to 4 servings

Here's a money-saving tip for you: pesto made with sunflower seeds instead of pine nuts or walnuts is far less expensive, and it's really quick to throw together for dinner, too. (You can also skip the avocados if they're expensive where you live.) Load the pasta up with your favorite steamed vegetables, or throw some extra garlic in the pesto if you know you're not gonna be kissing anyone. It's great warm or cold, especially topped with halved cherry tomatoes.

Ingredients:
1 pound of your favorite pasta
2 small avocados or 1 large avocado, peeled and pitted
½ cup packed fresh basil leaves
1 cup raw sunflower seeds (no shells)
1½ teaspoons minced garlic (about 3 small cloves)
2 tablespoons lemon juice
⅓ cup olive oil
½ teaspoon salt

Optional Additions:
¼ cup nutritional yeast added in step 2
1 cup of your favorite steamed veggies (I like broccoli) added in step 3

Optional Toppings:
1 cup halved cherry or grape tomatoes

Directions:
1. In a medium pot over medium-high heat, cook the pasta according to the directions on the package.
2. While the pasta cooks, put the avocados, basil, sunflower seeds, garlic, lemon juice, olive oil, and salt in a blender or food processor, and blend on high until smooth and creamy.
3. Drain the pasta once it's done. Return the pasta to the pot and add the pesto. Stir to coat the pasta evenly.

>> You can usually find raw sunflower seeds in the bulk section or next to the peanuts in the grocery aisle. Make sure you buy the kind without the shells.

TESTERS' TIPS:

>> "If you're omitting the avocado, you'll need to add more oil to make up for the natural oil the avocado would add." —Lisa K. from New Orleans, LA

MY TIPS:

JACKFRUIT CARNITAS TACOS

Yields 4 servings

I consider this recipe one of my greatest hits. It's inspired by a recipe I created for my first book, *The Super Easy Vegan Slow Cooker Cookbook*. That one proved to be so popular, I created this stovetop version.

Ingredients:
1 (20-ounce) can young green jackfruit, drained

½ cup diced red, white, or yellow onion (about ½ medium onion)

1 teaspoon minced garlic (about 2 small cloves)

½ tablespoon canola or vegetable oil (or 3 tablespoons water)

1 tablespoon ground cumin

½ tablespoon ground coriander

½ teaspoon ground cinnamon

1 teaspoon liquid smoke

½ cup water and ¼ vegetable bouillon cube, or ½ cup vegetable broth

8 corn tortillas

Optional Toppings:
1 avocado, sliced

1 handful chopped cilantro

Squeeze of lime juice

Hot sauce

Finely chopped onion

Directions:
1. Using your fingers, pull apart the jackfruit pieces into shreds and add them to a medium pan with a lid.
2. Place the pan over medium-high heat and add the onion, garlic, and oil (or water). Sauté for 2 minutes.
3. Add the cumin, coriander, cinnamon, liquid smoke, and water and bouillon cube (or broth) and mix well.
4. Turn the heat to high and bring the broth to a boil. Cover the pan and turn the heat down to low.
5. Simmer for 15 minutes.
6. Remove from the heat and divide into 8 equal portions, placing each into a corn tortilla. Serve with optional toppings or your favorite taco fixings.

>>If you find that your Jackfruit Carnitas have too much liquid, turn the heat up for 1 to 2 minutes or until it's absorbed.

TESTERS' TIPS:

>>"Toasting the tortillas on the stovetop makes these 1,000 percent better." —Lisa K. from New Orleans, LA

MY TIPS:

LENTIL AND SWEET POTATO BOWL

Yields 4 servings

Let me introduce you to the very first recipe that I created for PlantBasedMealPlan.com, a series of one-week meal plans I developed with Michelle Cehn. My goal was to write meal plans specifically showing how affordable plant-based eating could be. I'm super proud to say we've done our part in helping so many people realize how accessible and delicious plant-based eating can be. This recipe in particular has become a household staple for so many, and I couldn't be happier.

For the Lentils:

½ tablespoon canola or vegetable oil (or 3 tablespoons water)

½ cup diced red, white, or yellow onion (about ½ medium onion)

1½ teaspoons minced garlic (about 3 small cloves)

1 cup uncooked lentils, rinsed

2 cups water and 1 vegetable bouillon cube, or 2 cups vegetable broth

1 teaspoon ground cumin

For the Base:

1 cup chopped kale, steamed

1 cup cooked brown rice or quinoa (see page 226 or 224)

1 microwaved sweet potato (about 1 pound), diced (see page 238)

Directions:

1. In a medium saucepan over medium-high heat, heat the oil (or water). Add the onion and garlic and sauté for 3 minutes or until the onion becomes tender and translucent.

2. Add the lentils, water and bouillon cube (or broth), and cumin and mix thoroughly.

3. Bring to a boil and mix until the bouillon cube is dissolved, 1 to 2 minutes. Cover and reduce the heat to low. Simmer for 20 minutes or until the lentils are soft.

4. Meanwhile, in a pot with a steamer basket, bring water to a boil over medium-high heat. Place the kale in the basket and steam for 3 to 4 minutes or until it softens.
5. Layer the rice (or quinoa), kale, lentils, and sweet potatoes in bowls.

TESTERS' TIPS:

>>"If you don't have a steamer basket, steam the kale by heating it on a covered plate in the microwave for 1 to 2 minutes." —A.F. from Sacramento, CA

MY TIPS:

VEGGIE TOFU PASTA

Yields 6 to 8 servings

The inspiration for this pasta came from my friend Grace's meal plan on Plant-Based on a Budget. I had never had tofu in pasta, and it was a game changer for me. It adds a delicious, unique ricotta-like texture while boosting the protein. Win-win!

Ingredients:

1 pound of your favorite pasta

½ tablespoon canola or vegetable oil (or 3 tablespoons water)

½ cup diced red, white, or yellow onion (about ½ medium onion)

1½ teaspoons minced garlic (about 3 small cloves)

3½ cups packed chopped spinach

1 (14-ounce) block extra-firm tofu, pressed (see page 18)

2 teaspoons dried oregano

1 (25-ounce) jar marinara sauce

Optional Additions:

¼ cup frozen peas added in step 3

1 cup frozen broccoli florets added in step 2

Directions:

1. In a medium pot over medium-high heat, cook the pasta according to the directions on the package.

2. While the pasta cooks, begin the veggie sauce. In a large pot over medium-high heat, heat the oil (or water). Add the onion and garlic and sauté for 2 to 3 minutes or until the onion is tender and translucent. Add the spinach and let it wilt.

3. Using your fingers, crumble the tofu into the pot and cook for another 5 minutes.

4. Stir in the oregano. Add the marinara sauce and cook for 5 minutes.

5. While the sauce cools, check on the pasta. When it's cooked, remove from the heat and drain.

6. Divide the pasta into bowls and top with the sauce.

TONI'S TIPS:

>> You can keep the stems on your spinach. But if you choose to take them off, save them to add extra nutrients to your smoothies.

FRIED BROWN RICE

Yields 4 servings

I make a huge batch of brown rice nearly every week. On the third or fourth day, when my rice is getting a little tough, it's time to bust out this fried rice recipe. It's easily one of my favorite meals.

Ingredients:

1 tablespoon sesame oil

½ cup diced red, white, or yellow onion (about ½ medium onion)

1 teaspoon minced garlic (about 2 small cloves)

½ cup frozen peas

½ cup grated or finely diced carrots

2½ cups cooked brown rice (see page 226)

1½–2 tablespoons soy sauce

Optional Toppings:

1 tablespoon hot sauce

1 cup Fried Tofu (see page 246)

½ cup chopped unsalted roasted peanuts

Directions:

1. In a large pan over medium-high heat, heat the sesame oil. Add the onion, garlic, peas, and carrots and sauté for 3 minutes or until the onion is tender and translucent.

2. Add the cooked brown rice and soy sauce. Cook for 5 to 8 minutes, stirring frequently.

TONI'S TIPS:

>>I like my fried rice to be fried and crispy, so rather than stir, I let mine sit for a couple of minutes at a time, then flip over the rice using a spatula.

PEANUT BUTTER RAMEN STIR-FRY

Yields 4 servings

When I was younger, to save money, my grandma would make our stir-fries using Top Ramen noodles. Back then they were only ten cents a package! They're still ridiculously cheap today. If you don't want to use ramen noodles, feel free to use rice noodles or chow mein noodles. Remember to look for plant-based ramen. That said, this recipe doesn't use the flavor packet, just the noodles. There are also plenty of natural instant ramen brands that are fantastic and cheap, just not ten-cents cheap.

Ingredients:

3 (3-ounce) packages instant ramen noodles

½ tablespoon canola or vegetable oil (or 3 tablespoons water)

½ cup diced red, white, or yellow onion (about ½ medium onion)

1 teaspoon minced garlic (about 2 small cloves)

½ bell pepper, diced

1 cup frozen broccoli

½ cup grated or finely diced carrots

1 batch Peanut Sauce (see page 147)

Optional Additions:

1 cup shredded green cabbage, steamed, added in step 2

Directions:

1. In a medium pot over medium-high heat, cook the ramen noodles according to the directions on the package (do not use the flavoring packets).
2. While the noodles cook, begin on the sauce. In a large pan with a lid over medium-high heat, heat the oil (or water). Add the onion, garlic, and bell pepper and sauté for 3 minutes.
3. Add the broccoli and carrots. Cover and cook for another 3 to 5 minutes or until the veggies are tender.
4. Drain the noodles.
5. Add the noodles and peanut sauce to the pan of veggies. Mix until the noodles and veggies are coated.

TESTERS' TIPS:

>>"For extra nutrition, try doubling all the vegetables in this recipe." —Michelle R. from St. Paul, MN

CALZONES

Yields 3 to 4 calzones

My awesome friend Amy Galvan inspired this recipe. Back when I started learning to cook, she was an excellent source of ideas for easy, satisfying meals. She was the one who got me hip to calzones, and she'd make several batches and freeze them individually for her husband to take to work.

You can mix and match with your calzone filling, using whatever veggies you have in your fridge. And if you feel like splurging, you can also throw in some vegan "chick'n" or cheese.

Ingredients:

1 store-bought or homemade pizza
   dough (see page 240)
2 tablespoons flour (for dusting surfaces)
2 cups marinara sauce
½ cup chopped green or red bell
   pepper (about ½ bell pepper)
½ cup diced red, white, or yellow onion
   (about ½ medium onion)

1 (2.25-ounce) can sliced black olives,
   drained

Optional Additions:

4 vegan chick'n strips, baked and
   chopped, added in step 5
1 cup vegan cheese added in step 5
½ cup chopped cremini mushrooms
   added in step 5

Directions:

1. Preheat the oven to 425 degrees.
2. Divide the pizza dough into 3 or 4 balls, depending on the size of the calzones you'd like.
3. On a well-floured surface (I prefer using two baking sheets rather than my countertop), take each ball and roll it out into a circle.
4. Place ½ cup marinara sauce on the middle of each piece of dough, leaving a 1-inch space from the edge.
5. Place the bell pepper, onion, and olives over the sauce. Fold each piece of dough in half, fold the edges over, and pinch the edges together.
6. Bake for 15 to 20 minutes or until the calzones are golden brown. Remove from the oven and cool.

>>It's tasty to use barbecue sauce, vegan chick'n nuggets, diced red onion, and diced pineapple. You can also try it with Avocado Sunflower Seed Pesto (see page 151).

>>When I freeze the calzones, I place each one in a quart-size freezer bag. They keep for up to a month.

MY TIPS:

SPAGHETTI SQUASH WITH MARINARA AND VEGGIES

Yields 2 to 4 servings

Like many other healthy foods, spaghetti squash didn't make it onto my radar until I was well into my twenties. I love to use this as a lighter alternative to regular pasta—it's made from fresh produce and is equally satisfying.

Ingredients:
½ tablespoon canola or vegetable oil (or 3 tablespoons water)
½ green or red bell pepper, diced
½ cup diced red, white, or yellow onion
1 teaspoon minced garlic (about 2 small cloves)
2 cups chopped spinach
1 (14.5-ounce) can diced tomatoes with their juices
½ tablespoon dried oregano
1 (15-ounce) can black or pinto beans, drained and rinsed

¼ teaspoon salt
1 roasted spaghetti squash, cut in half (see page 238)

Optional Additions:
3 or 4 sliced cremini mushrooms added in step 1
½ teaspoon chopped fresh basil or dried basil added in step 2

Optional Garnishes:
½ tablespoon minced fresh parsley

Directions:
1. In a large pan over medium-high heat, heat the oil (or water). Add the bell pepper, onion, and garlic and sauté for 3 minutes or until the onion is tender and translucent.
2. Add the spinach, tomatoes, oregano, beans, and salt. Reduce the heat to low and simmer for 5 minutes.
3. While the veggies are cooking, scrape the inside of the roasted spaghetti squash until it resembles spaghetti strands.
4. Pour the pepper and tomato sauce over the spaghetti squash.

>>At some grocery stores, you can find canned diced tomatoes in Italian spices. That's a good option for making this even more flavorful.

>>For a thicker sauce, swap out the canned tomatoes for jarred marinara sauce.

MY TIPS:

STUFFED BELL PEPPERS

Yields 4 servings

These stuffed bell peppers are packed with protein and a mouthful of flavor. Make them even better by topping with homemade Cashew Cream (see page 249).

Ingredients:
4 green or red bell peppers
2 cups cooked quinoa (cooked in vegetable broth) (see page 224)
1 (15-ounce) can black or pinto beans, drained and rinsed
1 tablespoon taco seasoning
¼ teaspoon salt
1 (10-ounce) can red enchilada sauce

Optional Additions:
½ cup diced red, white, or yellow onion, sautéed, added in step 3
½ teaspoon minced garlic (about 1 small clove) added in step 3
½ cup corn kernels added in step 3

Optional Garnishes:
1 avocado, diced
1 cup vegan sour cream
1 cup Cashew Cream (see page 249)

Directions:
1. Preheat the oven to 400 degrees.
2. Cut the bell peppers in half lengthwise and remove the seeds. Place on a baking sheet.
3. In a medium bowl, combine the quinoa, beans, taco seasoning, and salt.
4. Spoon the quinoa mixture into the bell peppers.
5. Pour the enchilada sauce onto the baking sheet between the stuffed peppers.
6. Cover with aluminum foil and bake for 25 minutes.

TONI'S TIPS:
>>If you don't have taco seasoning, you can make your own simple version by adding 1 tablespoon cumin and 1 teaspoon chili powder.

TESTERS' TIPS:
>>"If you don't have enchilada sauce, I recommend adding marinara instead."
—Melanie S. from Warsaw, NY

VEGGIE CHOW MEIN

Yields 4 to 6 servings

By now, you know I'm on a mission to always make use of my veggies before they expire. When my spinach starts to droop or the carrots get a bit bendy, I like to turn to this recipe so I can clear out my fridge. Feel free to sub in any vegetables you need to use up, although if you make it by the book, it'll also be delicious.

Ingredients:

1 (8-ounce) package
   Asian-style noodles
   (like rice noodles,
   udon, or ramen)
1 tablespoon canola
   or vegetable oil (or 3
   tablespoons water)
1 cup thinly sliced celery
   (about 3 ribs)
½ cup diced red, white,
   or yellow onion (about
   ½ medium onion)
½ cup grated carrots
1 teaspoon minced garlic
   (about 2 small cloves)
½ cup vegetable broth
2 tablespoons soy sauce
1 cup bean sprouts

Optional Additions:

1 cup chopped green
   cabbage added in step 2
Hot sauce as a
   condiment

Directions:

1. In a large pot over medium-high heat, boil water and cook the noodles according to the directions on the package.
2. While the noodles are cooking, prepare the vegetables. In a large pan or wok, heat the oil (or water). Add the celery, onion, carrots, and garlic and sauté for 3 to 4 minutes or until the celery and onion are tender and the onion is translucent.
3. Add the broth and soy sauce. Bring to a boil, then turn down the heat and simmer for 5 minutes.
4. Add the cooked noodles and bean sprouts and mix thoroughly. Cook for 5 minutes, stirring occasionally.

TONI'S TIPS:

>>If you like yours a little saltier, add more soy sauce.
>>I recommend frying it a little longer until the noodles dry up a bit. Cook them for 2 extra minutes, then flip the noodles and cook for 2 more minutes.
>>If you don't like grating carrots, finely dicing them works just fine.

>>"A few leaves of bok choy chopped up, along with some sliced green onion, really make this dish burst with flavor." —Lisa O. from Sacramento, CA

MY TIPS:

TERIYAKI TOFU STIR-FRY

Yields 2 to 4 servings

I called this recipe a Teriyaki Tofu Stir-Fry, but it could easily be a Barbecue Stir-Fry or a Peanut Sauce Stir-Fry just by swapping out the sauce for another flavor. This is also an excellent way to empty out your fridge of any veggies, so feel free to mix it up in either direction.

Ingredients:

½ tablespoon canola or vegetable oil (or 3 tablespoons water)

⅔ cup finely chopped green or red bell pepper (about 1 small pepper)

½ cup diced red, white, or yellow onion (about ½ medium onion)

1 cup frozen chopped broccoli

1 teaspoon minced garlic (about 2 small cloves)

1 batch Fried Tofu (see page 246)

⅓ cup store-bought teriyaki sauce

Directions:

1. In a large pan, heat the oil (or water) over medium-high heat.

2. Add the bell pepper, onion, broccoli, and garlic and sauté for 3 minutes or until the onion is tender and translucent.

3. Add the Fried Tofu and evenly pour the teriyaki sauce on top.

4. Continue to cook on medium-high heat, flipping the tofu to coat it evenly, until the sauce is completely absorbed, 4 to 5 minutes.

MY TIPS:

SWEET POTATO SANDWICH

Yields 2 sandwiches

About a decade ago, I worked at an all-vegan restaurant in Sacramento that had a sandwich similar to this one. It was a customer favorite, and I loved it, too. It's been so long, I couldn't faithfully re-create that sandwich. But I think I've made a pretty darn amazing version of my own.

Ingredients:
1 microwaved small-medium sweet potato (see page 238)

½ tablespoon olive oil (or 3 tablespoons water)

½ cup diced red, white, or yellow onion (about ½ medium onion)

1½ teaspoons minced garlic (about 3 small cloves)

2 ciabatta rolls (or your favorite rolls)

1 avocado, sliced

1 tomato, sliced

½ head romaine lettuce, chopped, or 1 cup of sprouts

Optional Additions:
Vegan mayonnaise added in step 4

Dijon mustard added in step 4

Caramelized onions added in step 4

Directions:
1. Slice the sweet potato lengthwise into ½-inch slices.
2. In a medium pan over medium-high heat, heat the olive oil (or water). Add the onion and garlic and sauté for 3 minutes or until the onion becomes tender and translucent.
3. Add the sweet potato and mix so it can absorb the onion and garlic flavor. Cook for 1 to 2 minutes.
4. Cut the ciabatta rolls in half lengthwise. Top with the sweet potato mixture, avocado, tomato, and lettuce.

>>I like to cut the ciabatta rolls like they do at the sandwich shop, not going all the way through the bread, so the rolls hold together as a unit.

>>While I sauté the onion and garlic, I also like to throw the bread in the toaster oven for a few minutes.

TESTERS' TIPS:

>>"This is wonderful with caramelized onions." —Kathleen P. from Stockton, CA

MY TIPS:

GINGER LIME TOFU

Yields 2 to 4 servings

For many, many years, I thought tofu was straight-up nasty. It was gelatinous, flavorless, and blobby. It's only been in the last few years that I've learned how to properly cook and season tofu, which is the key to making it super flavorful. Now it's one of my favorite sources of protein. If you're still on the fence about tofu, this recipe will teach you to love it.

Ingredients:

¾ cup soy sauce

2–3 tablespoons lime juice, or to taste

2 tablespoons maple syrup or agave

1 tablespoon minced ginger

1 teaspoon minced garlic (about 2 small cloves)

2 batches Fried Tofu (see page 246)

Optional Toppings:

Cooked brown rice (see page 226)

Chopped green onion

Directions:

1. In a medium bowl, mix together the soy sauce, lime juice, maple syrup (or agave), ginger, and garlic.

2. In a large pan over medium-high heat, put down a single layer of Fried Tofu. Pour the soy sauce mixture on top.

3. Cook, flipping the tofu to coat it evenly, until the sauce is completely absorbed, 4 to 5 minutes.

TONI'S TIPS:

>>If you don't want to use the Fried Tofu recipe, you can sub in raw extra-firm tofu that's been pressed (see page 18).

MY TIPS:

TOFU VEGGIE GRAVY BOWL

Yields 4 servings

The base of this recipe is steamed vegetables and tofu. On busy nights, I'll microwave some frozen veggies, slice a block of raw tofu into cubes, and top it with the gravy. It's delicious. Feel free to swap out any veggies listed with the kind you already have in your fridge. If you're not familiar with how to steam veggies, see page 19.

For the Gravy:

2 tablespoons canola or vegetable oil (or 6 tablespoons water)

¼ cup diced red, white, or yellow onion

2 tablespoons whole wheat or all-purpose flour

1 cup water and 1 vegetable bouillon cube, or 1 cup vegetable broth

For the Veggie Base:

1 cup evenly sliced broccoli, steamed

1 cup evenly chopped zucchini, steamed

1 cup chopped carrots, steamed

½ (14-ounce) block extra-firm tofu, pressed and cut into ½-inch cubes (see page 18)

Directions:

1. In a medium pan over medium heat, heat the oil (or water) and onion and cook for 3 minutes or until the onion becomes tender and translucent.

2. Reduce the heat to low, add the flour, and stir until your roux has a smooth consistency, 2 to 3 minutes. It should resemble a paste.

3. Add the water and bouillon cube (or broth) and stir over low heat until the gravy thickens, 3 to 4 minutes.

4. On a plate, arrange the broccoli, zucchini, carrots, and tofu, and pour the gravy over this base. Serve immediately.

TONI'S TIPS:

>>It's best to use a very flavorful broth since that's where you'll be getting the most of your flavor.

TESTERS' TIPS:

>>"I'm gluten-free, so I use tapioca starch (easily found at Asian markets) instead of flour. You could also use arrowroot or gluten-free flour." —Rebecca T. from Phoenix, AZ

TOTCHOS

Yields 4 to 6 servings

Not familiar with Totchos? Let me introduce you. They're tater tots with nacho fixings. Tot-chos. And they are so flippin' good! I find them to be the perfect Friday night recipe. In my home, after a long work week, I'll put on a Disney feel-good movie and pile high the Totchos and their toppings. This is comfort food at its best.

Ingredients:

1 (32-ounce) bag frozen tater tots

1 batch Nacho Cheese (see page 96)

1 (15-ounce) can black beans, drained and rinsed

Optional Toppings:

1 avocado, diced

⅔ cup diced tomato

Dollop of Cashew Cream (see page 249) or vegan sour cream

1 tablespoon minced cilantro

Squeeze of lime juice

Directions:

1. Prepare the tater tots according to the directions on the package.

2. After they're baked, top with the Nacho Cheese and black beans. You can transfer the Totchos to a plate or save an extra dish by serving them directly from the pan once it cools.

MY TIPS:

DESSERTS

Transitioning to a plant-based diet can sound restrictive. But I wanted to prove in these pages that it doesn't have to be that way. Yes, salads and staples like lentils and brown rice can be part of a plant-based diet. So, too, can delicious desserts like cupcakes, ice cream, and milkshakes. In this chapter, I'll show you how it's done.

FOUR-INGREDIENT CHOCOLATE PIE

Yields 1 pie

This chocolate pie is one of the easiest I've ever made. There are only four ingredients, and all of them can be snapped up at your local grocery store. For vegan chocolate chips, look at the ingredients and make sure they don't say "contains milk." I usually buy the Trader Joe's or Guittard semisweet chocolate chips. For the piecrust, Keebler's graham-cracker crust is a good bet.

Ingredients:

- 1 (12-ounce) bag vegan semisweet chocolate chips
- 1 (14-ounce) block silken (also called "soft") tofu, drained
- 2 teaspoons vanilla extract
- 1 vegan graham-cracker piecrust

Optional Toppings:

Fresh berries

Coconut Whipped Cream (see page 213)

Directions:

1. In a small, microwave-safe bowl, microwave the chocolate chips for 45 seconds. Mix with a fork until smooth. (If the chocolate is still lumpy, microwave for 20-second intervals, mixing in between, until the chocolate is completely smooth.)
2. In a blender or food processor, blend the melted chocolate, tofu, and vanilla until creamy.
3. Pour the tofu-chocolate mixture into the piecrust and place in the freezer for 30 minutes or until the filling solidifies. The pie can be stored in the refrigerator for up to 5 days.

TONI'S TIPS:

>>If you don't have a graham-cracker piecrust handy, you can crumble your favorite cookies or graham crackers and pack them tightly into the bottom of an 8-inch pie dish. Then pour the tofu-chocolate mixture on top of the crumbs and place the pie in the freezer.

>>"To make your own piecrust, use a sleeve of graham crackers, which has roughly ten, and pulse them in a blender or food processer until they crumble. Add ½ cup vegan butter to the blender or food processer and blend together. Using your fingers, press the graham-cracker mixture into the baking sheet." —Lisa K. from New Orleans, LA

MY TIPS:

>>Loaf pans are usually about 9 × 5 inches, but you can actually bake this in any oven-safe container. Try a muffin tin (aka "cupcake tin") if you like smaller, portioned-out bites of banana bread. You'll just have to adjust the baking time to 30 minutes. It'll yield 12 muffins.

TESTERS' TIPS:

>>"I like to undercook this bread slightly so that it's soft in the middle. Since there are no real eggs, there's no worry!" —Aaron O. from Seattle, WA

MY TIPS:

DEPRESSION ERA CUPCAKES

Yields 12 cupcakes

In my early twenties, I got really into baking with my friend Jenn Wong. We held bake sales, made fancy birthday cakes, and even tackled a wedding cake for two other friends, Gabe and Gianna. These days I've moved on from fussy, elaborate projects to ultra-easy, minimalist baking.

This cupcake recipe is now one of the only proper cakes that I'll bake. Its history stems from the Great Depression, when eggs and milk were scarce, but it can hold its own against modern-day recipes. And I've added my own tweaks to bring it up to date.

Ingredients:

1½ cups whole wheat or all-purpose flour

¾–1 cup granulated sugar (depending on your sweet tooth)

3 tablespoons cocoa powder

1 teaspoon baking soda

½ teaspoon salt

1 teaspoon vanilla extract

1 teaspoon white or apple cider vinegar

5 tablespoons canola or vegetable oil

1 cup water

Optional Toppings:

Powdered sugar

Strawberry slices

Store-bought vegan frosting

Directions:

1. Preheat the oven to 350 degrees. Line a cupcake tin with paper baking cups.
2. In the bowl of an electric mixer (or in a large bowl, by hand), mix together all the ingredients until smooth.
3. Pour the batter into each baking cup until it's three-quarters full.
4. Bake for 15 to 20 minutes. Test a cupcake by sticking a toothpick in the middle. If the toothpick comes out dry, the cupcakes are done.

>>For the photo here, I used a store-bought vanilla frosting. There are plenty of options available for vegan frostings, and you might be surprised that almost all Pillsbury frostings are vegan.

MY TIPS:

COCONUT WHIPPED CREAM OVER BERRIES

Yields 6 to 8 servings

Fruit for dessert feels wholesome but also dull. Make it far more decadent by adding a big ol' dollop of whipped cream.

Ingredients:

1 (13.5-ounce) can full-fat coconut milk

1 teaspoon vanilla extract

3 teaspoons powdered sugar

4 cups fresh berries

Directions:

1. Place the can of coconut milk in the refrigerator and let it sit overnight or for at least 6 hours.

2. After the coconut milk is completely chilled, the milk and water should have separated. Remove the lid and pour out the water. (You can save it for a smoothie.)

3. In the bowl of an electric mixer, whisk the solidified coconut milk, vanilla, and powdered sugar on high for 5 minutes or until the mixture is fluffy. (If you don't have an electric mixer, a hand whisk will also work.)

4. Place the berries into small bowls and top each with a generous dollop of the whipped cream. Serve immediately.

TONI'S TIPS:

>>Try to avoid using coconut milk with guar gum because it prevents the milk from solidifying. If you can't find one that is full-fat and doesn't have guar gum, coconut cream also works.

MY TIPS:

PROTEIN CHOCOLATE CHIP COOKIES

Yields 12 cookies

Cookies don't have to be loaded up with fat and sugar. They can be filled with plant-based protein instead. This recipe makes for a great afternoon treat without the accompanying sugar slump. (That said, if you *do* want a cookie that's ultra-decadent, I've got you covered, too. Head to page 220 for the indulgent version.)

Ingredients:

1 teaspoon canola or vegetable oil (for greasing)

1 (15-ounce) can chickpeas, drained and rinsed

½ cup peanut butter (creamy or chunky)

1½ teaspoons vanilla extract

¼ teaspoon baking powder

⅛ teaspoon salt

¾ cup vegan semisweet chocolate chips

Directions:

1. Preheat the oven to 350 degrees, and lightly grease a baking sheet.
2. In a food processor or high-powered blender, blend the chickpeas, peanut butter, vanilla, baking powder, and salt until smooth.
3. Using a spoon, mix in the chocolate chips.
4. Scoop out 1 tablespoon cookie dough and roll the scoop into a tight ball. Place the ball on the prepared baking sheet and flatten using your fingertips. Repeat until all the cookie dough is used.
5. Bake for 20 minutes or until the cookies turn golden brown.

TONI'S TIPS:

>>For a sweeter cookie, you can add ¼ cup granulated sugar.

>>This recipe makes a small batch of cookies, and they're best eaten on the first day.

>>If you don't have a high-powered blender or food processor, you can mix the batter by hand. First mash the chickpeas, and then add the remaining ingredients.

PUMPKIN PIE

Yields 1 pie

Most people think of pumpkin pie as a Thanksgiving dish, but why limit yourself to just once a year? Pie this good should be appreciated all year round. To save on time, I usually purchase a premade piecrust. Marie Callender's frozen piecrusts are vegan and tasty. But if you're all about the DIY life, I included an easy recipe for you to follow on page 239.

Ingredients:
1 (15-ounce) can
   pumpkin purée
1 cup plant-based milk
½ cup granulated sugar
¼ cup all-purpose flour
½ tablespoon molasses
1 teaspoon vanilla extract
¼ teaspoon salt
1 tablespoon pumpkin
   pie spice
1 store-bought or
   homemade piecrust
   (see page 239)

Directions:
1. Preheat the oven to 425 degrees.
2. In a large bowl, thoroughly mix the pumpkin, milk, sugar, flour, molasses, vanilla, salt, and pumpkin pie spice.
3. Pour the filling into the piecrust.
4. Bake for 10 minutes, then lower the heat to 350 degrees and bake for another 50 minutes or until a toothpick or knife inserted near the center comes out clean.
5. Let the pie cool for at least 30 minutes before serving.

TONI'S TIPS:
>>When I was recipe testing for this recipe, I tried lots of different brands of canned pumpkin and decided that I liked Libby's best. When I tried organic brands, I found that the pumpkin was too wet. If you decide to use organic pumpkin anyway, just dab the moisture from the top of the pie.

MY TIPS:

ORANGE CREAMSICLES

Yields 6 popsicles

Most of my twenties were spent living in older homes that only had window air-conditioning units. That doesn't quite cut it when you've got 112-degree heat waves! That's when these popsicles become your best friend.

And as usual, you should feel free to improvise and add whatever frozen fruit you'd like. Try some blueberries or a handful of pineapple chunks. Yum!

On a side note, how cute is my little brother?

Ingredients:
2 frozen bananas
¾ cup plant-based milk
1¼ cups orange juice
1½ teaspoons vanilla
    extract

Directions:
1. In a blender, blend all the ingredients on high until thoroughly combined.
2. Pour the mixture into popsicle molds, place in the freezer, and freeze overnight or until entirely solid, about 8 hours.

TONI'S TIPS:
>>If you don't have popsicle molds, you can fill your ice cube trays, cover with aluminum foil, and pop toothpicks in each cube.
If you're having trouble getting the popsicle out of the mold, run the mold under warm water.

MY TIPS:

REAL-DEAL CHOCOLATE CHIP COOKIES

Yields 24 cookies

Welcome to the most decadent recipe in the book! I wanted to end the dessert chapter on a high note, and this is a true way to "treat yo' self." (If you're looking for something a bit less indulgent, you'll find it on page 214.)

Ingredients:

1 cup margarine, plus more for greasing

1 tablespoon flaxseed meal

3 tablespoons warm water

1 cup brown sugar

½ cup granulated sugar

1½ teaspoons vanilla extract

1 teaspoon baking soda

2¼ cups all-purpose flour

½ teaspoon salt

¾ cup vegan semisweet chocolate chips

Optional Additions:

½ cup chopped walnuts added in step 4

Directions:

1. Preheat the oven to 375 degrees, and grease a baking sheet.
2. In a small bowl, beat together the flaxseed meal and water for 1 minute. Place in the refrigerator for 5 minutes.
3. In a large bowl, beat together the brown sugar, granulated sugar, and margarine.
4. Mix in the flaxseed meal mixture, vanilla, baking soda, flour, and salt. Stir in the chocolate chips.
5. Scoop tablespoonfuls of the dough onto the prepared baking sheet.
6. Bake for 10 minutes or until the cookies are golden and crispy around the edges. Allow to cool before eating.

MY TIPS:

BACK TO BASICS

*Every week on my day off, I like to pick a few basic
pantry staples and prep them for the week ahead. That
way I can craft the week's meals around whatever is
ready to go. Here's how to get back to the basics.*

QUINOA

Yields 3 cups

Like many other plant-based staples, quinoa was unfamiliar to me until I became a vegetarian. I didn't even know how it was pronounced. "Queen-wah"? "Qui-no-ah"? I've since learned that there's a pretty heated debate around whether it's pronounced "keen-no-wah," "kin-wah," or "keen-wah" (my personal preference).

But however it's pronounced, I couldn't live without it. These days, I gobble it up for breakfast cooked in milk and topped with fruit and cinnamon (see page 43), eat it for lunch in a salad (see page 62), or enjoy it for dinner with some vegetables and tofu. It's a great ingredient to make on your meal-prep day and use throughout the week.

PRESSURE COOKER METHOD

Ingredients:
1 cup quinoa
1½ cups water or
   vegetable broth

Directions:
1. Rinse the quinoa in cold water using a fine-mesh strainer.
2. Put the quinoa and water (or broth) into the pressure cooker and cook on high pressure for 5 minutes.
3. Let the pressure out, remove the lid, and fluff the quinoa with a fork.
4. Store in an airtight container in the fridge for up to 5 days.

STOVETOP METHOD

Ingredients:
1 cup quinoa
2 cups water or
   vegetable broth

Directions:
1. Rinse the quinoa in cold water using a fine-mesh strainer.
2. Add the quinoa and water (or broth) to a medium pot with a lid.

3. Over high heat, bring to a boil.
4. Cover with the lid and reduce the heat to low.
5. Cook for 20 minutes.
6. Remove from the heat and fluff with a fork.
7. Store in an airtight container in the fridge for up to 5 days.

TONI'S TIPS:

>>Quinoa in its natural form has a really bitter taste. To get rid of it, use a fine-mesh strainer to rinse the quinoa. If you don't have one, you can use a coffee filter. In a pinch, I've covered my regular colander with a clean kitchen towel and rinsed the quinoa over the towel. (If you're like me when I started cooking and you have no idea what a colander is, it's also known as a strainer, and it's often used for draining cooked pasta.)

Quinoa can be cooked in liquids other than water. Sometimes when I want more flavor, I'll cook it in vegetable broth or I'll add half a bouillon cube to the water.

MY TIPS:

BROWN RICE

Yields 2 cups

I grew up in a mixed-culture home thanks to a Japanese grandfather and a Mexican grandmother, which gave me an appreciation for great rice. However, neither of those cultures uses brown rice, so I was never exposed to it. Once I tried it, I considered it an "acquired taste." I didn't love the different texture, but I continued to eat it as it's a healthier option. Now I love its nutty texture and I eat it all the time.

PRESSURE COOKER METHOD

Ingredients:
1 cup brown rice
2 cups water

Directions:
1. Put the rice and water into the pressure cooker and cook on high pressure for 20 minutes.
2. Let the pressure out, remove the lid, and fluff the rice with a fork.
3. Store in an airtight container in the fridge for up to 4 days.

STOVETOP METHOD

Ingredients:
1 cup brown rice
2 cups water

Directions:
1. Add the rice and water to a medium pot with a lid.
2. Over high heat, bring to a boil.
3. Cover with the lid and reduce the heat to low.
4. Cook for 40 minutes.
5. Remove from the heat and fluff with a fork.
6. Store in an airtight container in the fridge for up to 4 days.

TONI'S TIPS:

>>If you want a little more flavor, you can replace the water with vegetable broth or throw in a bay leaf.

MY TIPS:

BEANS

Yields 3 cups

There are so many different types of beans and methods for cooking them. To keep it easy, I'm only going to talk about the three beans that I use most often: black beans, chickpeas (also called garbanzo beans), and pinto beans, and I will give directions for cooking them all unseasoned and unsoaked. If you want to season them, I like putting in 1 teaspoon garlic, ½ cup diced onion, and a pinch of salt before I start to boil them. You can also add some minced jalapeño and cumin, or you can come up with your own spice blend to add.

PRESSURE COOKER METHOD

Ingredients:
1½ cups black beans, chickpeas, or pinto beans, rinsed
5 cups water

Directions:
1. Put the beans and water into the pressure cooker and cook on high pressure. Cooking time varies according to the type of bean: black beans take 40 minutes; chickpeas take 50 minutes; and pinto beans take 50 minutes.
2. Release the pressure and remove the lid.
3. Store in an airtight container in the fridge for up to 5 days.

STOVETOP METHOD

Ingredients:
1½ cups black beans, chickpeas, or pinto beans, rinsed
5 cups water

Directions:
1. Put the beans and water into a large pot with a lid.
2. Over high heat, bring to a boil.
3. Cover the pot with the lid and reduce the heat to low.

4. Simmer for 1½ to 3 hours on low heat. Check at 1½ hours, and if the beans are still tough, cover them with the lid again and simmer for 30 minutes more. Repeat until they are tender.
5. Store in an airtight container in the fridge for up to 5 days.

SLOW COOKER METHOD

Ingredients:

1½ cups black beans, chickpeas, or pinto beans, rinsed

5 cups water

Directions:

1. Put the beans and water into the slow cooker.
2. Cover and cook on low heat for 6 to 8 hours. Check at 6 hours. If the beans are still tough, cover them with the lid and continue to cook for another 30 minutes. Repeat until they are tender.
3. Store in an airtight container in the fridge for up to 5 days.

TONI'S TIPS:

>> Each can of beans is equal to about 1½ cups of cooked beans. I recommend making a big batch and freezing them in 1½-cup portions. They last for up to 3 months in the freezer.

>> If you have questions about eating beans and passing gas, I recommend checking out the article on NutritionFacts.org titled "Beans & Gas: Clearing the Air."

MY TIPS:

BROWN OR GREEN LENTILS

Yields 2½ cups

PRESSURE COOKER METHOD

Ingredients:

1 cup lentils, rinsed

1½ cups water or
   vegetable broth

Directions:

1. Put the lentils and water (or broth) into the pressure cooker and cook on high pressure for 8 minutes.
2. Release the pressure and remove the lid.
3. Store in an airtight container in the fridge for up to 5 days.

STOVETOP METHOD

Ingredients:

1 cup lentils, rinsed

1½ cups water or
   vegetable broth

Directions:

1. Put the lentils and water (or broth) into a large pot with a lid.
2. Over high heat, bring to a boil.
3. Cover the pot with the lid and reduce the heat to low.
4. Simmer for 30 minutes.
5. Store in an airtight container in the fridge for up to 5 days.

SLOW COOKER METHOD

Ingredients:

1 cup lentils, rinsed

4 cups water or
    vegetable broth

Directions:

1. Put the lentils and water (or broth) into the slow cooker.
2. Cover and cook on low heat for 6 to 8 hours. Check at 6 hours. If the lentils are still tough, cover them with the lid and continue to cook for another 30 minutes. Repeat until they are tender.
3. Store in an airtight container in the fridge for up to 5 days.

GREEN SPLIT PEAS

Yields 2 cups

Ingredients:

1 cup split peas, rinsed

1½ cups water

Directions:

1. Put the split peas and water into a large pot with a lid.
2. Over high heat, bring to a boil.
3. Cover the pot with the lid and reduce the heat to low.
4. Simmer for 45 minutes.
5. Store in an airtight container in the fridge for up to 5 days.

MY TIPS:

CROUTONS

Yields 4 servings

Ingredients:
½ day-old baguette, sliced
2 tablespoons olive oil
½ tablespoon garlic salt

Directions:
1. Preheat the oven to 350 degrees.
2. Brush the baguette slices with the olive oil and sprinkle with the garlic salt.
3. Cut the bread into cubes, place on a baking sheet, and bake for 10 to 15 minutes or until golden brown.
4. Allow the croutons to cool before serving.
5. The croutons are best if served immediately after baking.

MY TIPS:

STRAWBERRY DRESSING

Yields 1½ cups

During the summer, I can find one-pound cartons of strawberries for one dollar. It makes me giddy because I know that means I can use those cartons as an opportunity to experiment with strawberry *everything*, including this sweet and simple salad dressing.

Ingredients:
- 1½ cups chopped fresh strawberries
- 1–2 tablespoons agave, brown sugar, or maple syrup
- ½ tablespoon lemon juice

Directions:
1. In a food processor or blender, blend all the ingredients until smooth.
2. Store in an airtight container in the fridge for up to 7 days.

Optional Additions:
- 1–2 mint leaves (start with 1) added in step 1

MY TIPS:

APPLE CIDER VINAIGRETTE

Yields ½ cup

Ingredients:

2 tablespoons apple cider
vinegar

¼ cup olive oil

½ tablespoon Dijon
mustard

1 tablespoon agave,
maple syrup, or
granulated sugar

1 teaspoon minced garlic
(about 2 small cloves)

Pinch of salt

Freshly ground pepper,
to taste

Directions:

1. In a small bowl, whisk together all the ingredients until well combined.
2. Store in an airtight container in the fridge for up to 7 days.

MY TIPS:

TAHINI DRESSING

Yields ½ cup

Ingredients:

¼ cup tahini

1 teaspoon minced garlic (about 2 small cloves)

3 tablespoons lemon juice (about 1 small lemon)

1 tablespoon agave, maple syrup, or granulated sugar

1 teaspoon soy sauce

1 teaspoon ground cumin

1 tablespoon olive oil

1 tablespoon hot water

Pinch of salt and pepper

Directions:

1. In a small bowl, whisk together all the ingredients until well combined.
2. Store in an airtight container in the fridge for up to 7 days.

TONI'S TIPS:

>>If you find that your dressing is too thick, mix in hot water by the tablespoon until it's pourable.

MY TIPS:

POTATOES

Yields 1 cooked potato

This works for cooking either sweet potatoes or russet potatoes.

Ingredients:
1 medium potato (sweet or russet)

Directions:
1. Using a fork, poke holes all over the potato for ventilation.
2. Put the potato on a microwave-safe plate and microwave it for 2 minutes. Flip it over and microwave for 2 more minutes.
3. If the potato is not soft yet, microwave again in 1-minute increments until it's soft. Store in the refrigerator in an airtight container for up to 4 days.

TONI'S TIPS:
>>If you're using a smaller potato, start off at 1-minute per side.

ROASTED SQUASH

Yields 1 roasted squash

This works for both butternut squash and spaghetti squash.

Ingredients:
1 squash (butternut or spaghetti)

Directions:
1. Preheat the oven to 400 degrees.
2. Put the whole squash on a baking sheet and bake for 1 hour. Store in the refrigerator in an airtight container for up to 4 days.

PIECRUST

Ingredients:

1 cup all-purpose flour, plus more for rolling

½ teaspoon baking powder

¼ teaspoon salt

2 tablespoons canola or vegetable oil, plus more if storing dough for later

½ teaspoon lemon juice

3½ tablespoons plant-based milk

4 tablespoons water

Directions:

1. In a medium bowl, thoroughly mix all the ingredients with a wooden spoon until a ball of dough forms.

2. Wrap the dough in plastic wrap and refrigerate for 1 hour.

3. If using right away, dust a work surface with flour, place the chilled dough down, and roll it out into a thin, flat 11-inch circle using a lightly floured rolling pin. Transfer to a 9-inch pie dish. Fill with your choice of fillings and bake according to the recipe's instructions.

4. If not using right away, cover the exterior of the dough with 1 teaspoon (or less) oil to keep it from drying out. Place this lightly oiled ball of dough in a medium bowl and cover tightly with plastic wrap (or place the dough in an airtight container). Refrigerate for up to 7 days.

TONI'S TIPS:

>> You can also freeze the dough: just transfer it to a pie dish, tightly wrap the prepared piecrust in plastic wrap, and store in the freezer for up to 2 months.

MY TIPS:

LORA'S PIZZA DOUGH

Yields 1 pizza crust

Yes, you can find premade pizza dough that is vegan. Pillsbury makes one that comes in a blue tube. Trader Joe's has three flavors—plain, whole wheat, and spinach—and they're all vegan. But nothing tops your own fresh dough made from scratch. It's simple, inexpensive, and much tastier. This version comes to you from the kitchen of my friend Lora Silver, who is kind enough to share her recipe with my readers. Thanks, Lora!

Ingredients:

1 (¼-ounce) packet active dry yeast

1 tablespoon molasses

1 cup warm water

2 tablespoons olive oil, plus more if storing dough for later

2½ cups white whole wheat flour, plus more for kneading

¾ teaspoon salt

1 teaspoon garlic powder

2 teaspoons Italian seasoning (or any combination that you like of dried basil, oregano, and thyme)

Directions:

1. In a small bowl, dissolve the yeast and molasses in warm water. Let the mixture sit for 10 minutes or until it becomes foamy.

2. In another large bowl, mix together the olive oil, flour, salt, garlic powder, and Italian seasoning. Pour in the yeast mixture and combine to form a ball of dough.

3. Sprinkle flour onto a work surface. Remove the dough from the bowl and knead it with a little extra flour (enough so it doesn't stick). Let it sit for 10 minutes before using.

4. If not using right away, cover the exterior of the dough with 1 teaspoon (or less) olive oil to keep it from drying out. Place this lightly oiled ball of dough in a medium bowl and cover tightly with plastic wrap (or place the dough in an airtight container). Refrigerate for up to 7 days. When you remove the dough from the fridge, you can shape it into pizza crust right away. Alternatively, you can allow the dough to become more pliable and easy to shape by letting it sit at room temperature for 15 minutes.

>>This dough doesn't work just for pizzas. You can use it as the base for my yummy Calzones (see page 169).

>>If you want to bake the dough without the Calzone recipe, preheat your oven to 450 degrees, and cook the pizza for 15 to 20 minutes (depending on how crispy you like your crust).

>>"Optional freezing tip: wrap the dough tightly in plastic wrap, then with another layer of aluminum foil. Freeze for up to 3 months. Defrost in the refrigerator over-night or at least 12 hours prior to baking." —Lora S. from Cleveland, OH

MY TIPS:

VEGETABLE BROTH

Yields 9 cups

What I love most about making my own broth is that it reduces my food waste. Throughout the week, I set aside my veggie scraps and onion skins in an airtight container in the refrigerator or freezer (wherever there's more space), and then I throw them in with this recipe. As in many of my other recipes, you can sub in or out the veggies you have on hand. The result? A tasty and inexpensive broth.

Ingredients:

1 tablespoon canola or vegetable oil (or 3 tablespoons water)

1 red, white, or yellow onion, thinly sliced with skin

4 cloves garlic, crushed

3 celery ribs, thinly sliced

3 carrots, thinly sliced

¼ cup packed fresh parsley leaves

1 cup chopped kale

2 tablespoons soy sauce

9 cups water

1½ tablespoons peppercorns

1 tablespoon salt, or to taste

Optional Additions:

2–3 tablespoons tomato paste added in step 3

1 bay leaf added in step 3

3 tablespoons yellow or white miso added in step 3

1 vegetable bouillon cube added in step 3

Directions:

1. In a large pot with a lid, heat the oil (or water) over medium-high heat.
2. Add the onion, garlic, celery, and carrots and sauté for 3 to 4 minutes.
3. Add the parsley, kale, soy sauce, water, peppercorns, and salt.
4. Bring to a boil, reduce the heat to low, and cover the pot with a lid.
5. Simmer for 1 hour, then remove from the heat.
6. Once the liquid has cooled, strain the broth into a bowl using a colander. Press the vegetables to express their juices.
7. Store in an airtight container in the fridge for up to 7 days or in the freezer for up to 2 months.

PEANUT MILK

Yields 3 cups

Honestly, this recipe works really well with any type of nut, but I chose peanuts because they're the cheapest.

Ingredients:

1 cup unsalted roasted
  peanuts
¼ cup raisins
3 cups water

Optional Additions:

½ teaspoon vanilla
  extract added in step 2

Directions:

1. In a blender pitcher, soak the peanuts and raisins in the water. Let the mixture sit overnight or for at least 6 hours.
2. Blend the water, peanuts, and raisins together on high for 1 to 2 minutes.
3. Using cheesecloth or a mesh nut-milk bag, strain the milk into a pitcher, separating out the liquid from the solids.
4. Store in an airtight container in the fridge for up to 5 days.

MY TIPS:

FRIED TOFU

Yields 4 servings

This is my absolute, hands-down favorite way to make tofu. Freezing the tofu gives it a spongy texture and also allows it to soak up more flavor. It is seriously so good!

Ingredients:

1 (14-ounce) block extra-firm tofu

1½ tablespoons canola, vegetable, or sesame oil

Directions:

1. Place the package of tofu in the freezer overnight or for at least 4 hours.
2. Bring a pot of water to a boil. Remove the completely frozen tofu from its package and add it to the pot.
3. Boil the tofu for 10 minutes.
4. Remove the tofu from the pot to cool. When cool enough to handle, gently press the water out of the tofu with a clean kitchen towel. Be careful not to break the tofu.
5. Cut the tofu into ½-inch cubes.
6. In a large pan, heat the sesame oil over high heat. Once the oil is hot, add the tofu.
7. Fry the tofu for 1 to 2 minutes on each side or until it turns golden. When you're finished frying, place the tofu on a plate lined with a kitchen towel or paper towel to soak up the excess oil.
8. Store in an airtight container in the fridge for up to 5 days.

CASHEW CREAM

Yields 1½ cups

I realize that cashews are a bit pricey, so I didn't include them in any of the other recipes. But if you have some extra money to spend or have cashews in your pantry already, this cream makes a great topping for lots of the recipes in this book.

Ingredients:

1 cup raw cashews, soaked overnight and drained

½ cup water

¼ teaspoon salt

1–2 teaspoons lemon juice (depending on your sourness preference)

Directions:

1. In a blender or food processor, blend all the ingredients until creamy.
2. Store in an airtight container in the fridge for up to 7 days.

TONI'S TIPS:

>>Some stores with bulk sections sell "cashew pieces"—broken up cashews that are cheaper than their whole counterparts.

>>You can make this a sweet cream by omitting the salt and lemon juice and adding 1 tablespoon agave or maple syrup and 1 teaspoon vanilla extract.

MY TIPS:

TEMPEH BACON

Ingredients:

2 tablespoons soy sauce

1 tablespoon water

1 tablespoon maple syrup
or agave

½ tablespoon liquid
smoke

1 (8-ounce) package
tempeh (any variety)

1 tablespoon canola or
vegetable oil

Directions:

1. In a medium bowl, combine the soy sauce, water, maple syrup (or agave), and liquid smoke. Set aside.

2. Cut the tempeh block in half lengthwise and then slice it as thinly as possible.

3. In a large pan over high heat, heat the oil. Add the tempeh in a single layer and cook for 2 minutes. Flip and cook for 2 more minutes.

4. While the tempeh is still in the pan, add the liquid mixture and sauté the tempeh for 3 minutes. Flip and cook for 3 more minutes or until the liquid is absorbed.

5. The Tempeh Bacon is best if served immediately.

TONI'S TIPS:

>>I like to cook the tempeh for a couple of minutes longer to get it crispy and even a bit charred. It tastes more similar to bacon that way.

MY TIPS:

SAMPLE MEAL PLAN FOR ONE

About ten years ago, there was a social media movement called the SNAP Challenge. SNAP, standing for Supplemental Nutrition Assistance Program, is also commonly known as "food stamps." The goal of the challenge was to have influencers try to live off SNAP benefits while educating the public on how limited SNAP benefits could be when you have to feed a whole family.

Originally, I was intrigued by the idea of this challenge. I thought I'd find new resources to share with my audience. But as the challenge unfolded, I became completely disheartened by a lack of sensitivity among the influencers. I saw bloggers grinning in photos with cheap and unhealthy food at discount grocery stores. It seemed disrespectful to the people who are down-and-out and depend on this assistance. But it was that disappointment that led me to create the first Plant-Based on a Budget Meal Plan Challenge.

My message for the challenge was about saving money and eating healthier. I wanted it to serve as a resource for people who had very limited income, as well as people who were looking for cooking inspiration. My weekly food budget was twenty-five dollars per person per week, and there were three different free monthlong options based on how many people are in your family. Those are still on PlantBasedonaBudget.com and were so insanely popular that I was inspired to team up with Michelle Cehn from the blog *World of Vegan* to create the polished upgrade.

Together, Michelle and I have created meal plans that have helped thousands of people jump-start their plant-based journey while also saving them some money in the process. I hope these meal plans can help you, too. This is a brief sample of what we offer digitally on PlantBasedMealPlan.com. I've kept the budget to thirty dollars per person per week.

GROCERY SHOPPING LIST

NOTE: This does not include oil, salt, or pepper

Produce

1 medium tomato (any variety)

1 bunch cilantro

2 medium lemons

4 medium red, white, or yellow onions

1–2 heads garlic (10 small cloves)

6 bananas

1 bunch kale or spinach

1 small green or red bell pepper

1 (½-inch) piece ginger

6 large carrots

1 large russet potato

1 carton cherry tomatoes

Bulk

3 cups old-fashioned rolled oats

1 cup uncooked lentils

6 tablespoons raw sunflower seeds (no shells)

1 tablespoon ground cumin

1 teaspoon chili powder

2 cups brown rice

Other

2 (15-ounce) cans pinto beans

1 (15-ounce) can black beans

1 (15-ounce) can chickpeas

1 (15-ounce) can unsalted corn

1 (12-ounce) package frozen berries (any variety)

1 (12-ounce) package frozen chopped broccoli

½ gallon plant-based milk

1 packet taco seasoning

1 (10-ounce) bottle teriyaki or other stir-fry sauce

1 (6-count) package vegetable bouillon cubes

1 (30-count) bag corn tortillas

2 (14-ounce) blocks extra-firm tofu

1 (15.5-ounce) bottle green or red salsa

1 pound shaped pasta (bowties, rigatoni, penne, etc.)

1 (6.5-ounce) jar marinated artichoke quarters

DAY ONE

Breakfast: Overnight Oats
Lunch: Bean and Corn Salad
Dinner: Lentil Tacos

DAY TWO

Breakfast: Green Banana Smoothie
Lunch: Lentil Tacos leftovers
Dinner: Teriyaki Tofu Stir-Fry + Brown Rice

DAY THREE

Breakfast: Overnight Oats
Lunch: Teriyaki Tofu Stir-Fry + Brown Rice leftovers
Dinner: Carrot Ginger Soup

DAY FOUR

Breakfast: Green Banana Smoothie
Lunch: Bean and Corn Salad leftovers
Dinner: Lentil Tacos leftovers

DAY FIVE

Breakfast: Chilaquiles
Lunch: Carrot Ginger Soup leftovers
Dinner: Perfect Potluck Pasta Salad

DAY SIX

Breakfast: Chilaquiles leftovers
Lunch: Carrot Ginger Soup leftovers
Dinner: Bean and Corn Salad leftovers

DAY SEVEN

Breakfast: Overnight Oats
Lunch: Tacos made with Chilaquiles leftovers (or other leftovers)
Dinner: Perfect Potluck Pasta Salad leftovers

SOME TIPS:

- Prep Overnight Oats for day one and three. You can prep the serving for day seven after day four.

- Prepare smoothie fixings (minus the milk) by putting the ingredients in a freezer bag or airtight container and sticking them in the freezer until you're ready to use them. That way, in the morning, all you need to do is dump the frozen ingredients in a blender and add the milk.

- If you want to save even more money, use dried beans instead of whole (see page 228). Keep in mind that ¾ cup dried beans cook up to the equivalent of about one 15-ounce can.

- For the Teriyaki Tofu Stir-Fry, you can swap out the teriyaki sauce to whatever sauce you have on hand or is cheapest at the grocery store.

- Make a big batch of brown rice, and you'll have it handy to add ½-cup portions to any meal of your choosing.

ACKNOWLEDGMENTS

First and foremost, thank you to my parents, George and Lisa Okamoto, who have shown me what hard work looks like. I'm forever grateful for the long hours you worked to get me here, and I will spend every day of my life trying to make the most of the opportunities you've given me.

And thank you to my family—Gabriel Okamoto, Elena Deras, Jolene and Larry Shapiro—who will always show up for me in good times and in bad. I feel like the most privileged woman to be born into such a loving and loyal, ride-or-die group of people.

Paul Shapiro, love of my life, thank you for the inspiration, the love, the space to create, the time to collaborate, and for the truly wonderful partnership you've created with me. I couldn't have done this book and this work without you and your support. And I can't wait to do it again and again forever.

Michelle Cehn, if it wasn't for you, who knows what I'd be doing? You encouraged me to make Plant-Based on a Budget my life's work. I'll never be able to fully express the importance of your encouragement. Thank you for being the best business partner in the world.

A huuuuuge thank you to the entire team who helped create this book: To my agents, Jaidree Braddix and Celeste Fine, for walking alongside me through this entire process. My publisher, Glenn Yeffeth at BenBella, for believing in my idea and my brand. To Leah Wilson, Maria Hart, and

Jennifer Greenstein, for all the highly detailed work and finesse you put into my manuscript—you've made me really proud of this book. To my food photographer, Jenny Love, for traveling to Sacramento from Denver to take my gorgeous recipe photos (and allowing me to listen to the entire Taylor Swift discography in the process). To Sarah Avinger and the design team, Monica Lowry in production, Heather Butterfield in marketing, and everyone else at BenBella who has worked on my book along the way, for your help in making this dream project come to life. I'm so filled with gratitude.

Finally, thank you to my army of recipe testers: Grace Amico, Justin Au, Toube Benedetto, Cathy Bradford, Max Broad, Gianna Cannataro, Hannah Carrol, Angie Cooper, Isabelle Cnudde, Alex and Holly Evans-Peterson, Lyssa Everett, Annemieke Farrow, Josh Fernandez, Mary Kaye Ferreter, Jodie Foreman, Caryn Ginsberg, Debbie Hart, Kathryn Harvey, Holly Jackson, Logan Jeffrey, Tamaron Johnson, Lisa Kurtz, Virginia Guzman Loenberg, Susan Malphurs, Vannesa Manriquez, Shaunna Martin, Roxane Masson, Katie Metraux, Johanna Miller, Lisa Okamoto, Kathleen Peebles, Jennifer Piccolo, Idalia Ramos, Robin Ritchie, Michelle Rosier, Michelle Salemi, Paul Schwartz, Jolene Shapiro, Paul Shapiro, Erica Shultz, Lora Silver, Matthew Smith, Sarah Smith, Melanie Swanson, Tyler Tiznado, Rebecca Tuohino, Laura vanZandt, Andrea Waybright, Anna Wetherbee, Brett Young, Irene Zhan, and Brian Zimmer. It's your feedback that helped create such a tasty book.

Lastly, thank you to anyone who has ever written a recipe or an article for Plant-Based on a Budget, fixed my site when it's crashed (hi, Justin Lewis!), or shared my resources with someone.

This book really is a dream come true.

METRIC CONVERSIONS

Key

tsp = teaspoon

tbsp = tablespoon

dsp = dessert spoon

US standard	UK
¼ tsp	¼ tsp (scant)
½ tsp	½ tsp (scant)
¾ tsp	½ tsp (rounded)
1 tsp	¾ tsp (slightly rounded)
1 tbsp	2½ tsp
¼ cup	¼ cup minus 1 dsp
⅓ cup	¼ cup plus 1 tsp
½ cup	⅓ cup plus 2 dsp
⅔ cup	½ cup plus 1 tbsp
¾ cup	½ cup plus 2 tbsp
1 cup	¾ cup and 2 dsp

SUBJECT INDEX

money-saving tips, 7–13

other bills and, 3

for Plant-Based on a Budget Meal Plan Challenge, 253–254

for vegans, 4, 5

food processor, 6

food stamps, 253

"Free Formed Bread," 12

freezer bags, 9

freezing

bananas, 18

leftovers, 11

produce, 9

sauces, 13

friends

cooking with, 10

meal swapping with, 17

frozen vegetables, 11, 18–19

fruits

freezing, 9

staples, 21–22

fruit trees, 13

G

gardening, 13

garlic, jarred, 18

garlic press, 18

grains, rinsing, 19

grocery shopping

affordable, 5

money-saving tips for, 7–13

organizing list for, 16

for sample meal plan, 254–255

H

herbs

growing, 13

storing, 11–12

How Not to Die (Toni Okamoto), ix

hypertension, x

I

Instant Pot, 6, 15

K

kitchen

equipment for, 6, 14, 15, 17

organization of, 17–18

knives, 6, 17

L

leftovers, 11, 15–16

M

meal plan(s)

buying only what you need for, 12

creating, 18

grocery shopping list for, 254–255

for one, sample, 253–256

on PlantBasedMeal Plan.com, 254

tips for, 256

weekly menus, 255

meal swapping, 17

measurement

metric conversions, 259

when buying ingredients, 7

metric conversions, 259

money-saving tips, 7–13

O

oils, swapping water for, 19

P

pepper, 20

Plant-Based on a Budget

kitchen equipment for, 6

Meal Plan Challenge, 253–254

origin of, 4

recipes for, 5–6

pots, 6

poverty, risks associated with, ix–x

prepared foods

in grocery story, 8

at home, 8–9

pressing tofu, 18–19

pressure cookers, 15
prices
    at cashier, watching, 13
    per ounce, 9
    on post-holiday items, 13
    sale items, 9–11
produce. *see also* fruits; vegetables
    discounted, 8
    at farmers' markets, 8
    freezing, 9
    freezing sauces made from, 13

R
recipes
    My Tips for, 20
    swapping ingredients in, 5
    Testers' Tips for, 5–6, 20
    using water instead of oil in, 19
repurposing food, 11
rinsing beans/grains, 19

S
SAD (standard American diet), ix
sale items, 9–11
salt, 20
sauces, freezing, 13
shopping list, 8
slow cookers, 15
SNAP (Supplemental Nutrition Assistance Program), 253
spices
    bulk bins of, 8
    staples, 22
splurges, 11, 22
standard American diet (SAD), ix
staples, 21–22
steaming vegetables, 19–20
storage containers, 6
store brands, 9
Supplemental Nutrition Assistance Program (SNAP), 253

T
Testers' Tips, 5–6, 20
time-saving tips, 14–18
tips
    money-saving, 7–13
    My Tips for recipes, 20

Testers' Tips, 5–6, 20
time-saving, 14–18
tofu, pressing, 18–19

U
utensils, 6

V
veganism
    author's journey toward, 2–3
    others' attitudes toward, 4
vegetable broth, making, 19
vegetables
    freezing, 9
    frozen, 11, 18–19
    preparing double batches of, 16
    staples, 21–22
    steaming, 19–20
    unpeeled, 16–17
Vitamix, 6

W
World of Vegan blog, 254

RECIPE INDEX

ABOUT THE AUTHOR

TONI OKAMOTO is the founder of Plant-Based on a Budget, the popular website, food blog, and meal plan that shows readers how to save dough by eating veggies. She's also author of *The Super Easy Vegan Slow Cooker Cookbook* and cohost of *The Plant-Powered People Podcast* and the *Business for Good Podcast*. Plant-Based on a Budget has been featured in *Reader's Digest*, *U.S. News and World Report*, and other publications and on NBC News. Toni is also a regular presence on the Fox affiliate in Sacramento, where she teaches viewers how to break their meat-eating habit without breaking their budget. Toni is a burrito enthusiast and spends her free time swing dancing across the county.

Download a **FREE** digital copy of
BenBella's Best of Plant-Based Eating
and sign up for more exclusive offers and info at

BENBELLAVEGAN.COM

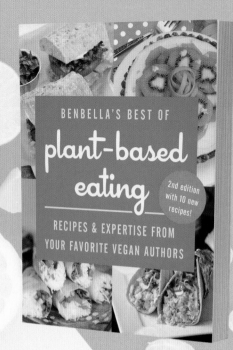

WITH NEARLY 50 RECIPES FROM

The China Study cookbook series | Lindsay S. Nixon's The Happy Herbivore series

Chef Del Sroufe's *Better Than Vegan* | Christy Morgan's *Blissful Bites*

Heather Crosby's *YumUniverse* | Tracy Russell's *The Best Green Smoothies on the Planet*

Dreen Burton's *Plant-Powered Families* | Jeff and Joan Stanford's *Dining at The Ravens*

Eric Brent and Glen Merzer's *The HappyCow Cookbook*

Laura Theodore's *Jazzy Vegetarian Classics* | Christina Ross' *Love Fed*

Kim Campbell's *The PlantPure Nation Cookbook*

AND SELECTIONS FROM

T. Colin Campbell and Howard Jacobsons' *Whole* and *The Low-Carb Fraud*

Dr. Pam Popper and Glen Merzer's *Food Over Medicine*

J. Morris Hicks' *Healthy Eating, Healthy World* | Lani Muelrath's *The Plant-Based Journey*